Ground Beef Recipes

Jean Paré

www.companyscoming.com
visit our website

Front Cover

1. Caribbean Beef Salad, page 120
2. Chili Gumbo, page 75
3. Spinach-Stuffed Meatloaf, page 98

Props courtesy of:
Danesco Inc.
Pier 1 Imports

Back Cover

1. Leek-Crowned Beef Pie, page 46
2. Ricotta Swiss Wedges, page 97
3. Cheeseburger Pie, page 58

Props courtesy of:
Casa Bugatti
Cherison Enterprises Inc.
Pyrex® Bakeware

We gratefully acknowledge the following suppliers for their generous support of our Test and Photography Kitchens:

Broil King Barbecues
Corelle®

Hamilton Beach® Canada
Lagostina®

Proctor Silex® Canada
Tupperware®

Ground Beef Recipes

Copyright © Company's Coming Publishing Limited

All rights reserved worldwide. No part of this book may be reproduced, stored in a retrieval system or transmitted in any form by any means without written permission in advance from the publisher.

In the case of photocopying or other reprographic copying, a license may be purchased from the Canadian Copyright Licensing Agency (Access Copyright). Visit www.accesscopyright.ca |or call toll free 1-800-893-5777. In the United States, please contact the Copyright Clearance Centre at www.copyright.com or call 978-646-8600.

Brief portions of this book may be reproduced for review purposes, provided credit is given to the source. Reviewers are invited to contact the publisher for additional information.

Eighth Printing April 2008

Library and Archives Canada Cataloguing in Publication
Paré, Jean, date
Ground beef recipes / Jean Paré.
(Original series)
Includes index.
ISBN 978-1-896891-83-5
1. Cookery (Beef). I. Title. II. Series.
TX749.5.B43P373 2006   641.6'62   C2005-905320-8

Published by
Company's Coming Publishing Limited
2311 – 96 Street
Edmonton, Alberta, Canada T6N 1G3
Tel: 780-450-6223 Fax: 780-450-1857
www.companyscoming.com

Company's Coming is a registered trademark owned by
Company's Coming Publishing Limited

We acknowledge the financial support of the Government of Canada through the Book Publishing Industry Development Program (BPIDP) for our publishing activities.

Printed in China

Want cooking secrets?

Six *"sneak preview"* recipes are featured online *with every new book released.*

Visit us at
www.companyscoming.com

Company's Coming Cookbooks

Original Series

- Softcover, 160 pages
- 6" x 9" (15 cm x 23 cm) format
- Lay-flat plastic comb binding
- Full-colour photos
- Nutrition information

Quick & easy recipes! Everyday ingredients!

Practical Gourmet Series

- Hardcover, 224 pages
- 8" x 10" (21 cm x 26 cm) format
- Full-colour throughout
- Nutrition information

Most Loved Recipe Collection

- Hardcover, 128 pages
- 8 3/4" x 8 3/4" (22 cm x 22 cm) format
- Durable sewn binding
- Full-colour throughout
- Nutrition information

Special Occasion Series

- Softcover, 176 pages
- 8 1/2" x 11" (22 cm x 28 cm) format
- Full-colour throughout
- Nutrition information

See page 157 for more cookbooks.
For a complete listing, visit
www.companyscoming.com

Table of Contents

Appetizers

Burgers

Casseroles

Chilies & Sauces

Meatballs

Sandwiches

Soups & Salads

Stovetop

The Company's Coming Story

Jean Paré (pronounced "jeen PAIR-ee") grew up understanding that the combination of family, friends and home cooking is the best recipe for a good life. From her mother, she learned to appreciate good cooking, while her father praised even her earliest attempts in the kitchen. When Jean left home, she took with her a love of cooking, many family recipes and an intriguing desire to read cookbooks as if they were novels!

"Never share a recipe you wouldn't use yourself."

When her four children had all reached school age, Jean volunteered to cater the 50th anniversary celebration of the Vermilion School of Agriculture, now Lakeland College, in Alberta, Canada. Working out of her home, Jean prepared a dinner for more than 1,000 people, launching a flourishing catering operation that continued for over 18 years. During that time, she had countless opportunities to test new ideas with immediate feedback— resulting in empty plates and contented customers! Whether preparing cocktail sandwiches for a house party or serving a hot meal for 1,500 people, Jean Paré earned a reputation for great food, courteous service and reasonable prices.

As requests for her recipes increased, Jean was often asked the question, "Why don't you write a cookbook?" Jean responded by teaming up with her son, Grant Lovig, in the fall of 1980 to form Company's Coming Publishing Limited. The publication of *150 Delicious Squares* on April 14, 1981 marked the debut of what would soon become one of the world's most popular cookbook series.

The company has grown since those early days when Jean worked from a spare bedroom in her home. Today, she continues to write recipes while working closely with the staff of the Recipe Factory, as the Company's Coming test kitchen is affectionately known.

There she fills the role of mentor, assisting with the development of recipes people most want to use for everyday cooking and easy entertaining. Every Company's Coming recipe is kitchen-tested before it is approved for publication.

Jean's daughter, Gail Lovig, is responsible for marketing and distribution, leading a team that includes sales personnel located in major cities across Canada. Company's Coming cookbooks are distributed in Canada, the United States, Australia and other world markets. Bestsellers many times over in English, Company's Coming cookbooks have also been published in French and Spanish.

Familiar and trusted in home kitchens around the world, Company's Coming cookbooks are offered in a variety of formats. Highly regarded as kitchen workbooks, the softcover Original Series, with its lay-flat plastic comb binding, is still a favourite among readers.

Jean Paré's approach to cooking has always called for quick and easy recipes using everyday ingredients. That view has served her well. The recipient of many awards, including the Queen Elizabeth Golden Jubilee Medal, Jean was appointed Member of the Order of Canada, her country's highest lifetime achievement honour.

Jean continues to gain new supporters by adhering to what she calls The Golden Rule of Cooking: *Never share a recipe you wouldn't use yourself.* It's an approach that has worked—millions of times over!

Foreword

If we peek into the freezer of a typical family home, we're sure to find a pound of ground. Whether it's hamburgers or meat sauce, shepherd's pie or cabbage rolls, we just can't get enough. We even sing about it—surely that poor meatball in "On Top of Spaghetti" deserves a better end!

Convenient, economical and versatile, ground beef is a menu mainstay. Think back to Mom's special Monday-night meatloaf or Uncle Harry's famous, eye-watering chili. And a young person moving away from home will often stuff at least one good skillet-supper recipe inside that box of hand-me-down dishes.

Ground Beef Recipes celebrates the versatility of this popular ingredient, and offers fresh ideas to tempt your friends and family. From Cheeseburger Pie and Salsa Porcupines to Roquefort Beef Tarts and Blue Moon Dumplings, the recipes include kid-pleasers as well as elegant company fare. And with dishes such as Sloppy Joe Tacos and Tandoori Chili, there's a range of tastes from the familiar to the exotic.

Fans of slow cookers will find two delicious ideas on these pages. On busy days, our Bolognese Sauce and Porcupine Stew will make coming home a pleasure when these inviting meals are waiting.

Many of the recipes featured here can be frozen. Make a double batch of our Tasty Meatballs, freeze the extras on a cookie sheet until firm, and pop them into a resealable freezer bag. Do this with our patties too! And remember that you can scramble-fry large quantities of ground beef and freeze in amounts suitable for recipes.

Any of the oven-cooked casseroles, chilies, meat sauces, meatloaves and dairy-free soups can also be frozen. Wrap each item securely or place in airtight containers. Use freezer-to-oven dishes to get supper on the table in no time.

Our tips for proper handling, storage and cooking of ground beef will help you take advantage of this delicious meal option. Explore the new kitchen-tested flavours we developed for *Ground Beef Recipes* and discover your favourites!

Jean Paré

Nutrition Information Guidelines

Each recipe is analyzed using the most current version of the Canadian Nutrient File from Health Canada, which is based on the United States Department of Agriculture (USDA) Nutrient Database.

- If more than one ingredient is listed (such as "hard margarine or butter"), or if a range is given (1 – 2 tsp., 5 – 10 mL), only the first ingredient or first amount is analyzed.

- For meat, poultry and fish, the serving size per person is based on the recommended 4 oz. (113 g) uncooked weight (without bone), which is 2 – 3 oz. (57 – 85 g) cooked weight (without bone)—approximately the size of a deck of playing cards.

- Milk used is 1% M.F. (milk fat), unless otherwise stated.

- Cooking oil used is canola oil, unless otherwise stated.

- Ingredients indicating "sprinkle," "optional," or "for garnish" are not included in the nutrition information.

Margaret Ng, B.Sc. (Hon.), M.A.
Registered Dietitian

Ground Beef Hints & Tips

Labelling

Canadian government standards regulate the labelling of ground beef, which is packaged according to fat content:

Extra-Lean:	no more than 10% fat
Lean:	no more than 17% fat
Medium:	no more than 23% fat
Regular:	no more than 30% fat

American regulatory standards require a lean/fat description on the label. The leanest choice is 95% lean/5% fat.

A Healthy, Economical Choice

Our test kitchen used lean and extra-lean ground beef for *Ground Beef Recipes*. But if there's a sale on regular or medium ground, don't limit your options! You can cut the fat content by draining cooked ground beef.

Those with specific dietary needs can further reduce total fat by placing drained, scramble-fried ground beef in a colander and rinsing with hot water.

Depending on your personal tastes and grocery budget, you may prefer to use regular or medium ground beef for some recipes, and lean or extra-lean for others. Generally, all types of ground beef can be used interchangeably; however, for best results:

• Use lean and extra-lean ground beef for fillings and meatloaves, where drippings are difficult to drain.

• Regular and medium ground beef can be used for burgers and meatballs, where fat will drip away during cooking, or for scramble-frying to use in chilies, soups and sauces, where fat is drained before adding other ingredients.

Cooking Tips

No matter which type of ground beef you use, the following tips will ensure that your dishes always taste their best:

• Gently mix ground beef with other ingredients until combined. Overmixing results in dense, heavy burgers and meatloaves.

• Shape patties and meatballs in uniform sizes for even cooking.

• To prevent the loss of juices that keep patties moist, turn them over only once, halfway through cooking time, and avoid pressing them with a spatula.

Cooking Methods for Patties

Recipes in this book use a variety of cooking methods for ground beef patties. These methods are interchangeable. If you have a favourite way to cook your patties, use it! Just follow the cooking times in the recipe, and remember to test for doneness, as indicated on page 9.

• To use a gas barbecue, preheat to medium. Place patties on greased grill.

• To use an electric grill, preheat for 5 minutes. Place patties on greased grill.

• To broil, place patties on a greased broiler pan on centre rack in oven.

• To pan-fry, heat 2 tsp. (10 mL) cooking oil in a large frying pan on medium.

Ground Beef Safety

Because the surface area of ground beef is greater than that of whole cuts, ground beef is more susceptible to harmful bacteria when handled or exposed to work surfaces. From the moment you place ground beef in your shopping cart, follow these food safety rules:

- Separate ground beef from fresh produce in your shopping cart and grocery bags, and keep it cool when transporting it home. Refrigerate or freeze ground beef within two hours of purchase.

- Store fresh (not previously frozen) uncooked ground beef in the refrigerator at 40°F (4°C) for up to 24 hours or in the freezer at 0°F (-18°C) for up to three months from the "packaged on" date.

- Ground beef labelled "previously frozen" should not be refrozen. Store in the refrigerator and use within 24 hours of purchase, or cook completely before refreezing. Fully cooked ground beef may be stored in the refrigerator for up to two days or in the freezer for at least three months.

- Always thaw frozen ground beef on a plate in the refrigerator, and never at room temperature. The plate will prevent drippings from contaminating fresh produce and other foods. Ground beef may be thawed in the microwave when it is cooked immediately afterward, or cooked from frozen when scramble-frying.

Testing for Doneness

- Ground beef is fully cooked when it reaches 160°F (71°C). Even when a patty, meatball or meatloaf is no longer pink inside, it may not be completely cooked. Test and be sure with a good-quality, digital meat thermometer that provides an exact temperature reading, and not just a doneness range. (The no-longer-pink indicator works for scramble-frying because all surfaces of the ground beef are cooked.)

- Remove meatloaves, meatballs and patties from heat before testing. Insert the thermometer into a loaf's centre layer of beef, or into the centre of the thickest part of the patty or meatball. Do not insert into stuffings or fillings. Check more than one item for doneness as hot and cold spots in your oven or barbecue may cause food to cook unevenly.

Glorious Ground Beef

Ground beef provides 12 essential nutrients, including zinc, niacin and B vitamins, and is an excellent source of protein.

Pastry Pinwheels

Mildly spiced, rich pastry swirls around beef and bubbling cheese. Sharp cheese is used for best flavour.

All-purpose flour	1 1/2 cups	375 mL
Paprika	1/2 tsp.	2 mL
Cayenne pepper	1/4 tsp.	1 mL
Salt	1/4 tsp.	1 mL
Cold hard margarine (or butter), cut up	1/2 cup	125 mL
Ice water	3 tbsp.	50 mL
Large egg	1	1
Fine dry bread crumbs	2 tbsp.	30 mL
Dried basil	1/4 tsp.	1 mL
Dried oregano	1/8 tsp.	0.5 mL
Dried thyme	1/8 tsp.	0.5 mL
Extra-lean ground beef	1/2 lb.	225 g
Grated sharp Cheddar cheese	1/2 cup	125 mL

Combine first 4 ingredients in medium bowl. Cut in margarine until mixture resembles coarse crumbs. Slowly add water, stirring with fork until mixture starts to come together. Do not overmix. Turn out pastry onto work surface. Shape into slightly flattened disc. Wrap with plastic wrap. Chill for 30 minutes.

Combine next 5 ingredients in large bowl.

Add ground beef and cheese. Mix well. Roll out pastry between 2 sheets of waxed paper to 8 x 16 inch (20 x 40 cm) rectangle (see Note). Discard top sheet of waxed paper. Press beef mixture evenly on top of pastry, leaving 1/2 inch (12 mm) edge on both long sides. Roll up tightly from 1 long side, jelly-roll style, using waxed paper as guide. Press seam against roll to seal. Cut into 1/2 inch (12 mm) slices. Arrange, cut-side up, about 1 inch (2.5 cm) apart on parchment paper-lined baking sheet. Bake in 400°F (205°C) oven for about 20 minutes until pastry is golden, and internal temperature of beef reaches 160°F (71°C). Makes 32 pinwheels.

1 pinwheel: 78 Calories; 4.9 g Total Fat (2.7 g Mono, 0.4 g Poly, 1.5 g Sat); 13 mg Cholesterol; 5 g Carbohydrate; trace Fibre; 3 g Protein; 75 mg Sodium

Pictured on page 17.

Note: To keep the bottom sheet of waxed paper from moving while rolling out the pastry, dampen the work surface underneath.

Cheeseburger Puffs

Kids and adults alike will love these bite-size, cheesy puffs.
Serve with barbecue or honey mustard sauce for dipping.

Cooking oil	1 tsp.	5 mL
Lean ground beef	1/2 lb.	225 g
All-purpose flour	1/2 cup	125 mL
Garlic powder	1/4 tsp.	1 mL
Onion powder	1/4 tsp.	1 mL
Salt	1/8 tsp.	0.5 mL
Water	1/2 cup	125 mL
Hard margarine (or butter), cut up	1/4 cup	60 mL
Large eggs	2	2
Grated medium Cheddar cheese	1/2 cup	125 mL
Finely chopped green onion	2 tbsp.	30 mL
Pepper	1/4 tsp.	1 mL

Heat cooking oil in medium frying pan on medium. Add ground beef. Scramble-fry for about 10 minutes until no longer pink. Drain. Set aside.

Combine next 4 ingredients in small cup.

Heat and stir water and margarine in heavy medium saucepan on high until boiling and margarine is melted. Reduce heat to medium. Add flour mixture all at once. Stir vigorously for about 1 minute until mixture pulls away from side of saucepan to form soft dough. Remove from heat. Let stand for 5 minutes.

Add eggs 1 at a time to dough, beating after each addition until well combined. Dough will be thick and glossy.

Add beef and remaining 3 ingredients. Mix well. Drop, using about 1 tbsp. (15 mL) for each, about 2 inches (5 cm) apart onto greased baking sheets. Bake in 425°F (220°C) oven for 15 to 17 minutes until golden. Let stand on baking sheets for 5 minutes before removing to wire racks to cool. Makes about 36 puffs.

1 puff: 41 Calories; 2.9 g Total Fat (1.5 g Mono, 0.3 g Poly, 0.9 g Sat); 17 mg Cholesterol;
2 g Carbohydrate; 0 g Fibre; 2 g Protein; 41 mg Sodium

Roquefort Beef Tarts

*Tender pastry holds a mellow blue cheese and
beef filling—perfect with a glass of red wine.*

Cooking oil	1 tsp.	5 mL
Lean ground beef	1/2 lb.	225 g
Crumbled Roquefort cheese	3/4 cup	175 mL
Finely chopped green onion	2/3 cup	150 mL
Large eggs	3	3
Milk	1/3 cup	75 mL
Sour cream	1/3 cup	75 mL
Salt	1/8 tsp.	0.5 mL
Pepper	1/8 tsp.	0.5 mL
Frozen mini tart shells, thawed	36	36

Heat cooking oil in medium frying pan on medium. Add ground beef.
Scramble-fry for about 10 minutes until no longer pink. Remove from
heat. Drain.

Add cheese and onion. Stir. Set aside.

Beat next 5 ingredients with whisk in medium bowl until well combined.

Arrange tart shells on 2 ungreased baking sheets. Spoon beef mixture
into shells. Pour egg mixture over top until full. Bake on separate racks in
375°F (190°C) oven for about 25 minutes, switching position of baking
sheets at halftime, until pastry is golden and egg mixture is set. Makes
36 tarts.

*1 tart: 81 Calories; 5.4 g Total Fat (2.3 g Mono, 0.6 g Poly, 2.2 g Sat); 25 mg Cholesterol;
5 g Carbohydrate; 0 g Fibre; 3 g Protein; 136 mg Sodium*

Pictured on page 17.

Nachos With Avocado Salsa

Great nibblies for a party or for a halftime snack during the big game. Add a bowl of sour cream to the tray before serving.

AVOCADO SALSA		
Large tomatoes, seeds removed, finely chopped	2	2
Ripe medium avocado, finely chopped	1	1
Finely chopped red onion	1/4 cup	60 mL
Lemon juice	1 tbsp.	15 mL
Garlic clove, minced (or 1/4 tsp., 1 mL, powder)	1	1
Salt	1/4 tsp.	1 mL
Cooking oil	1 tsp.	5 mL
Lean ground beef	1 lb.	454 g
Can of red kidney beans, rinsed and drained	19 oz.	540 mL
Medium salsa	1 1/2 cups	375 mL
Chopped red pepper	1 cup	250 mL
Bag of tortilla chips	11 1/4 oz.	320 g
Grated medium Cheddar cheese	1 1/2 cups	375 mL

Avocado Salsa: Combine first 6 ingredients in medium bowl. Makes about 2 cups (500 mL) salsa.

Heat cooking oil in large frying pan on medium. Add ground beef. Scramble-fry for about 10 minutes until no longer pink. Drain.

Add next 3 ingredients. Stir. Cook for about 10 minutes, stirring often, until red pepper is tender-crisp.

Arrange tortilla chips close together on ungreased baking sheet. Scatter beef mixture over top. Sprinkle with cheese. Broil on centre rack in oven for about 2 minutes until cheese is melted. Serve with Avocado Salsa. Serves 10 to 12.

1 serving: 392 Calories; 22 g Total Fat (10.5 g Mono, 2.2 g Poly, 7.4 g Sat); 42 mg Cholesterol; 33 g Carbohydrate; 6 g Fibre; 18 g Protein; 529 mg Sodium

Beefy Potato Cups

A bit fussy to make, but a delight for meat-and-potato lovers.
These may be prepared in the morning and chilled.
Pop them in the oven just before guests arrive.

Baby potatoes	12	12
Water		
Ice water		
Bacon slice, diced	1	1
Lean ground beef	1/4 lb.	113 g
Finely chopped onion	1/3 cup	75 mL
Grated medium Cheddar cheese	1/4 cup	60 mL
Sour cream	2 tbsp.	30 mL
Mayonnaise	1 tbsp.	15 mL
Steak sauce	1 tbsp.	15 mL
Chopped fresh chives (or 3/4 tsp., 4 mL, dried)	1 tbsp.	15 mL
Pepper, just a pinch		
Grated medium Cheddar cheese	1/3 cup	75 mL
Chopped fresh chives, for garnish		

Cook potatoes in water in large saucepan until tender-crisp. Drain. Immediately plunge into large bowl of ice water. Let stand for about 5 minutes until cold. Drain. Cut each potato in half lengthwise. Trim thin slice from bottom of each half. Using small spoon, scoop out potato flesh from halves, leaving 1/4 inch (6 mm) thick shells. Finely chop potato flesh. Reserve 1/2 cup (125 mL). Keep any remaining potato flesh for another use.

Cook bacon in small frying pan on medium until almost crisp.

Add ground beef and onion. Scramble-fry for about 10 minutes until beef is no longer pink. Drain.

Add reserved potato flesh and next 6 ingredients. Stir. Arrange potato shells on greased baking sheet. Fill with beef mixture.

(continued on next page)

Sprinkle with second amount of cheese. Bake in 350°F (175°C) oven for about 10 minutes until beef mixture is heated through and cheese is melted. Remove to large serving platter.

Garnish with chives. Makes 24 potato cups.

1 potato cup: 42 Calories; 2.2 g Total Fat (0.8 g Mono, 0.2 g Poly, 1 g Sat); 6 mg Cholesterol; 4 g Carbohydrate; trace Fibre; 2 g Protein; 39 mg Sodium

Pictured on page 17.

Artichoke Beef Dip

Ooey, gooey, cheesy dip for crackers, bread or veggie sticks.

Cooking oil	1 tsp.	5 mL
Lean ground beef	1/2 lb.	225 g
Garlic clove, minced (or 1/4 tsp., 1 mL, powder)	1	1
Chili powder	1/2 tsp.	2 mL
Ground coriander	1/4 tsp.	1 mL
Can of artichoke hearts, drained and chopped	14 oz.	398 mL
Mayonnaise	1 cup	250 mL
Sour cream	1 cup	250 mL
Grated Monterey Jack With Jalapeño cheese	1/2 cup	125 mL
Grated Parmesan cheese	1/2 cup	125 mL
Thinly sliced green onion	1 tbsp.	15 mL

Heat cooking oil in medium frying pan on medium. Add next 4 ingredients. Scramble-fry for about 10 minutes until ground beef is no longer pink. Drain. Transfer to large bowl.

Add next 5 ingredients. Stir. Spread evenly in greased 1 quart (1 L) casserole. Bake, uncovered, in 350°F (175°C) oven for about 30 minutes until heated through.

Sprinkle with onion. Makes about 4 cups (1 L).

1/4 cup (60 mL): 190 Calories; 17.5 g Total Fat (8.4 g Mono, 4.2 g Poly, 4.3 g Sat); 28 mg Cholesterol; 3 g Carbohydrate; 1 g Fibre; 6 g Protein; 216 mg Sodium

Homemade Snack Sausage

A firm, lean roll that will remind you of summer sausage.
Great garlic flavour. Serve with cheese and crackers.

Water	2 tbsp.	30 mL
Curing salt (not coarse salt)	2 tbsp.	30 mL
Liquid smoke	2 tsp.	10 mL
Onion powder	1 tsp.	5 mL
Dry mustard	1/2 tsp.	2 mL
Garlic powder	1/2 tsp.	2 mL
Pepper	1/2 tsp.	2 mL
Lean ground beef	1 lb.	454 g
Lean ground pork	1 lb.	454 g

Combine first 7 ingredients in large bowl.

Add ground beef and pork. Mix well. Divide into 2 equal portions. Roll each portion into 2 inch (5 cm) diameter log. Wrap each log tightly with heavy-duty foil. Chill for 24 hours. Using fork, poke holes in foil on top and bottom of logs. Set on broiler pan or on wire rack set on baking sheet with sides. Bake in 300°F (150°C) oven for 2 hours. Let stand in foil until cooled. Chill. Each roll cuts into 32 slices, for a total of 64 slices.

1 slice: 26 Calories; 1.6 g Total Fat (0.7 g Mono, 0.1 g Poly, 0.6 g Sat); 8 mg Cholesterol;
0 g Carbohydrate; 0 g Fibre; 3 g Protein; 227 mg Sodium

Pictured on page 17.

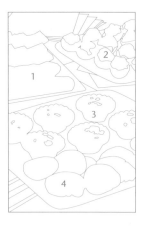

1. Homemade Snack Sausage, above
2. Beefy Potato Cups, page 14
3. Roquefort Beef Tarts, page 12
4. Pastry Pinwheels, page 10

Props courtesy of: Danesco Inc.

Appetizers

Blue Moon Dumplings

You'll want to serve these crispy, deep-fried dumplings more than once in a
blue moon! Blue cheese and basil add delicious flavour to the beef filling.

Large egg	1	1
Crumbled blue cheese	1/3 cup	75 mL
Chopped fresh basil (or 3/4 tsp., 4 mL, dried)	1 tbsp.	15 mL
Pepper	1/4 tsp.	1 mL
Extra-lean ground beef	1/2 lb.	225 g
Round dumpling wrappers	30	30
Large egg, fork-beaten	1	1
Cooking oil, for deep-frying		

Combine first 4 ingredients in medium bowl.

Add ground beef. Mix well.

Spoon about 2 tsp. (10 mL) beef mixture onto centre of 1 wrapper. Brush 1/2 of edge with second egg. Fold wrapper over beef mixture. Pinch edges to seal. Place on waxed paper-lined baking sheet. Cover with damp tea towel to prevent drying. Repeat to make 30 dumplings.

Deep-fry dumplings in small batches in hot (375°F, 190°C) cooking oil for about 2 minutes until wrapper is golden, and internal temperature of beef reaches 160°F (71°C). Remove to paper towels to drain. Makes 30 dumplings.

1 dumpling: 68 Calories; 4 g Total Fat (2 g Mono, 0.8 g Poly, 0.9 g Sat); 27 mg Cholesterol; 5 g Carbohydrate; trace Fibre; 3 g Protein; 76 mg Sodium

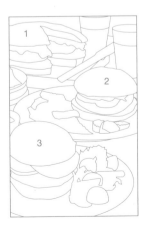

1. Giant Biscuit Burger, page 24
2. Presto Pesto Burgers, page 21
3. Teriyaki Burgers, page 22

Props courtesy of: Pfaltzgraff Canada
Tupperware®
Wiltshire®

Gouda Burgers

Horseradish adds delicious flavour to these cheesy burgers.

Large egg	1	1
White (or brown) bread slice, processed into crumbs	1	1
Finely chopped onion	1/2 cup	125 mL
Prepared horseradish	1 tbsp.	15 mL
Worcestershire sauce	1 tbsp.	15 mL
Salt	1/4 tsp.	1 mL
Pepper	1/8 tsp.	0.5 mL
Lean ground beef	1 lb.	454 g
Smoked Gouda cheese slices	4	4
HORSERADISH MAYONNAISE		
Mayonnaise	1/4 cup	60 mL
Dijon mustard (with whole seeds) or prepared mustard	1 tbsp.	15 mL
Chopped fresh chives (or 3/4 tsp., 4 mL, dried)	1 tbsp.	15 mL
Prepared horseradish	1 tbsp.	15 mL
Multi-grain rolls, split and toasted	4	4
Honey ham slices, halved	2	2
Tomato slices	8	8

Combine first 7 ingredients in large bowl.

Add ground beef. Mix well. Divide into 4 equal portions. Shape into patties to fit rolls. Place on greased broiler pan or on greased wire rack set on greased baking sheet with sides. (For other cooking methods, see page 8.) Broil on centre rack in oven for 5 to 7 minutes per side until fully cooked, and internal temperature of beef reaches 160°F (71°C).

Top patties with cheese slices. Broil for another 3 to 4 minutes until cheese is melted.

Horseradish Mayonnaise: Combine first 4 ingredients in small bowl. Makes about 6 tbsp. (100 mL).

Spread each roll with Horseradish Mayonnaise. Serve patties, topped with ham and tomato slices, in rolls. Makes 4 burgers.

1 burger: 592 Calories; 35.6 g Total Fat (15.6 g Mono, 5.5 g Poly, 11.9 g Sat); 164 mg Cholesterol; 29 g Carbohydrate; 3 g Fibre; 39 g Protein; 1151 mg Sodium

Presto Pesto Burgers

Work magic in the kitchen with these tantalizing burgers.
The aroma of basil and garlic makes them especially appealing.

Large egg	1	1
White (or brown) bread slice, processed into crumbs	1	1
Finely chopped onion	1/2 cup	125 mL
Grated Parmesan cheese	1/4 cup	60 mL
Basil pesto	2 tbsp.	30 mL
Garlic clove, minced (or 1/4 tsp., 1 mL, powder)	1	1
Lean ground beef	1 lb.	454 g
BASIL MAYONNAISE		
Mayonnaise	1/4 cup	60 mL
Basil pesto	2 tbsp.	30 mL
Onion (or hamburger) buns, split and toasted	4	4
Roasted red peppers, drained, blotted dry, cut into strips	1 1/4 cups	300 mL
Shaved Parmesan cheese	1/2 cup	125 mL
Chopped fresh basil (optional)	2 tbsp.	30 mL

Combine first 6 ingredients in large bowl.

Add ground beef. Mix well. Divide into 4 equal portions. Shape into 5 inch (12.5 cm) diameter patties. Preheat gas barbecue to medium. (For other cooking methods, see page 8.) Cook patties on greased grill for 5 to 7 minutes per side until fully cooked, and internal temperature of beef reaches 160°F (71°C). Transfer to large plate. Cover to keep warm.

Basil Mayonnaise: Combine mayonnaise and pesto in small bowl. Makes about 6 tbsp. (100 mL).

Spread each bun with Basil Mayonnaise. Serve patties, topped with remaining 4 ingredients, in buns. Makes 4 burgers.

1 burger: 593 Calories; 35.9 g Total Fat (16.9 g Mono, 6.5 g Poly, 10 g Sat); 135 mg Cholesterol; 31 g Carbohydrate; 2 g Fibre; 35 g Protein; 796 mg Sodium

Pictured on page 18.

Teriyaki Burgers

The grilled pineapple slices made this recipe an
instant hit when it first appeared in The Beef Book.

Reserved pineapple juice	1/4 cup	60 mL
Steak sauce	3 tbsp.	50 mL
Soy sauce	2 tbsp.	30 mL
Finely grated, peeled gingerroot	1 1/2 tsp.	7 mL
(or 1/4 tsp., 1 mL, ground ginger)		
Sesame seeds, toasted (see Tip,	1 1/2 tsp.	7 mL
page 129)		
Lean ground beef	1 lb.	454 g
Chopped fresh bean sprouts	1 cup	250 mL
Green onions, thinly sliced	2	2
Canned pineapple slices, drained and	4	4
juice reserved		
Hamburger buns, split	4	4

Combine first 5 ingredients in small bowl. Measure 1/4 cup (60 mL) into medium bowl. Set aside remaining pineapple juice mixture as basting sauce.

Add next 3 ingredients to pineapple juice mixture in medium bowl. Mix well. Divide into 4 equal portions. Shape into 1/2 inch (12 mm) thick patties. Preheat gas barbecue to medium. (For other cooking methods, see page 8.) Cook patties on greased grill for 5 to 7 minutes per side, brushing with basting sauce, until fully cooked, and internal temperature of beef reaches 160°F (71°C). Transfer to large plate. Cover to keep warm.

Blot pineapple slices with paper towels. Cook on greased grill for 2 to 3 minutes per side until heated through.

Serve patties, topped with pineapple slices, in buns. Makes 4 burgers.

1 burger: 361 Calories; 12.8 g Total Fat (5.6 g Mono, 1.1 g Poly, 4.4 g Sat); 57 mg Cholesterol; 35 g Carbohydrate; 2 g Fibre; 26 g Protein; 987 mg Sodium

Pictured on page 18.

Green Chili Burgers

Lime and Chinese five-spice powder give these burgers a subtle Asian flavour. Top with hoisin or plum sauce and garnish with fresh bean sprouts or suey choy.

Large egg	1	1
Fine dry bread crumbs	1/2 cup	125 mL
Can of diced green chilies	4 oz.	113 g
Sour cream	2 tbsp.	30 mL
Grated lime zest	1 tsp.	5 mL
Lime juice	1 tsp.	5 mL
Chinese five-spice powder	1/2 tsp.	2 mL
Salt	1/2 tsp.	2 mL
Garlic powder	1/4 tsp.	1 mL
Lean ground beef	1 lb.	454 g
Sesame hamburger buns, split	6	6

Combine first 9 ingredients in large bowl.

Add ground beef. Mix well. Divide into 6 equal portions. Shape into 4 inch (10 cm) diameter patties. Preheat gas barbecue to medium. (For other cooking methods, see page 8.) Cook patties on greased grill for 5 to 7 minutes per side until fully cooked, and internal temperature of beef reaches 160°F (71°C).

Serve patties in buns. Makes 6 burgers.

1 burger: 302 Calories; 10.7 g Total Fat (4.6 g Mono, 0.9 g Poly, 3.9 g Sat); 76 mg Cholesterol; 30 g Carbohydrate; 2 g Fibre; 20 g Protein; 573 mg Sodium

Paré Pointer
Vampires are such a pain in the neck.

Giant Biscuit Burger

This plate-sized novelty burger will impress the kids. A hearty sandwich for the guys on game night, too. You can use the dough to make smaller biscuits to serve with meatloaf or meatballs.

GIANT BISCUIT

All-purpose flour	2 cups	500 mL
Baking powder	4 tsp.	20 mL
Granulated sugar	2 tsp.	10 mL
Salt	1/2 tsp.	2 mL
Milk	3/4 cup	175 mL
Cooking oil	1/4 cup	60 mL
Fine dry bread crumbs	1/2 cup	125 mL
Italian dressing	1/3 cup	75 mL
Seasoned salt	1 tsp.	5 mL
Parsley flakes	1 tsp.	5 mL
Lean ground beef	1 lb.	454 g
Mayonnaise	1/4 cup	60 mL
Sweet pickle relish	1/4 cup	60 mL
Large tomato slices	6 – 8	6 – 8
Thinly sliced onion	1/4 cup	60 mL
Grated medium Cheddar cheese	1/2 cup	125 mL
Green leaf lettuce leaves	3	3

Giant Biscuit: Combine first 4 ingredients in large bowl. Make a well in centre.

Add milk and cooking oil to well. Stir until just moistened. Turn out dough onto lightly floured surface. Knead 8 to 10 times. Roll or pat out to 8 inch (20 cm) diameter circle. Place on greased baking sheet. Bake in 425°F (220°C) oven for about 15 minutes until golden. Cool. Makes 1 biscuit.

Combine next 4 ingredients in medium bowl.

Add ground beef. Mix well. Roll into ball. Place on ungreased 12 inch (30 cm) pizza pan or on baking sheet with sides. Pat out to 9 inch (22 cm) diameter patty. Bake for about 15 minutes until fully cooked, and internal temperature of beef reaches 160°F (71°C). Transfer to large plate. Cover to keep warm.

(continued on next page)

Burgers & Patties

Cut biscuit in half horizontally. Spread mayonnaise on top half. Spread relish on bottom half.

Layer tomato slices, onion and cheese, in order given, on top of relish. Carefully slide patty onto cheese. Top with lettuce. Cover with top half of biscuit. Cuts into 8 wedges.

1 wedge: 499 Calories; 29 g Total Fat (14.7 g Mono, 7.2 g Poly, 5.4 g Sat); 48 mg Cholesterol; 42 g Carbohydrate; 3 g Fibre; 18 g Protein; 908 mg Sodium

Pictured on page 18.

Borscht Burgers

Baba would be proud! Tasty patties with a Ukrainian influence.
Excellent topped with Horseradish Mayonnaise, page 20.

Large egg	1	1
Milk (or water)	2/3 cup	150 mL
Crushed buttery crackers	1/2 cup	125 mL
Finely chopped onion	1/2 cup	125 mL
Potato flakes	1/3 cup	75 mL
Grated fresh beets	1/3 cup	75 mL
Dill weed	1/2 tsp.	2 mL
Salt	1 tsp.	5 mL
Pepper	1/4 tsp.	1 mL
Lean ground beef	1 lb.	454 g
Cooking oil	2 tsp.	10 mL
Hamburger buns, split	6	6

Combine first 9 ingredients in large bowl.

Add ground beef. Mix well. Divide into 6 equal portions. Shape into 4 inch (10 cm) diameter patties.

Heat cooking oil in large frying pan on medium. (For other cooking methods, see page 8.) Add patties. Cook for 5 to 7 minutes per side until fully cooked, and internal temperature of beef reaches 160°F (71°C).

Serve patties in buns. Makes 6 burgers.

1 burger: 333 Calories; 13.3 g Total Fat (6 g Mono, 1.9 g Poly, 4 g Sat); 75 mg Cholesterol; 32 g Carbohydrate; 2 g Fibre; 20 g Protein; 773 mg Sodium

Jalapeño Popper Burgers

Cheese-filled, breaded and deep-fried jalapeño peppers are known as "poppers."
Now you can enjoy spicy popper flavour in a burger stuffing!

Crushed seasoned croutons	1/2 cup	125 mL
Block of cream cheese, softened	4 oz.	125 g
Sliced pickled jalapeño peppers, chopped	2 – 3 tsp.	10 – 15 mL
Ground cumin	1/4 tsp.	1 mL
Garlic powder	1/4 tsp.	1 mL
Seasoned croutons	1/4 cup	60 mL
Crushed seasoned croutons	1/3 cup	75 mL
Finely chopped onion	1/4 cup	60 mL
Worcestershire sauce	1 tsp.	5 mL
Chili powder	1/4 tsp.	1 mL
Lean ground beef	1 lb.	454 g
Salsa	1/4 cup	60 mL
Pickled jalapeño pepper slices	12 – 16	12 – 16
Hamburger buns, split	4	4

Put first amount of crushed croutons into small shallow dish.

Beat next 4 ingredients in small bowl. Add whole croutons. Stir. Divide into 4 equal portions. Shape into 3 to 4 inch (7.5 to 10 cm) diameter patties. Press both sides of each cheese patty into crushed croutons until coated. Set aside.

Combine next 4 ingredients in large bowl.

Add ground beef. Mix well. Divide into 8 equal portions. Shape into 5 inch (12.5 cm) diameter patties. Place each cheese patty between 2 beef patties. Pinch edges to seal. Arrange on greased broiler pan or on greased baking sheet with sides. (For other cooking methods, see page 8.) Broil on centre rack in oven for 5 to 7 minutes per side until fully cooked, and internal temperature of beef reaches 160°F (71°C).

Serve patties, topped with salsa and jalapeño pepper slices, in buns. Makes 4 burgers.

1 burger: 544 Calories; 27.8 g Total Fat (11 g Mono, 1.9 g Poly, 12.5 g Sat); 92 mg Cholesterol; 43 g Carbohydrate; 3 g Fibre; 30 g Protein; 804 mg Sodium

Burgers & Patties

Chipotle Jerk Burgers

Don't be intimidated by the long list of ingredients—they all work together to create the delicious "jerk" flavour of these smoky burgers.

Thinly sliced green onion	1/2 cup	125 mL
Fine dry bread crumbs	1/3 cup	75 mL
Chipotle chili pepper in adobo sauce, chopped (see Tip, page 74)	1	1
Frozen concentrated orange juice, thawed	2 tbsp.	30 mL
Soy sauce	2 tbsp.	30 mL
Finely grated, peeled gingerroot (or 3/4 tsp., 4 mL, ground ginger)	1 tbsp.	15 mL
Brown sugar, packed	1 tbsp.	15 mL
Garlic clove, minced (or 1/4 tsp., 1 mL, powder	1	1
Dried crushed chilies	1/2 tsp.	2 mL
Dried thyme	1/2 tsp.	2 mL
Ground allspice	1/2 tsp.	2 mL
Ground cinnamon	1/4 tsp.	1 mL
Ground cloves	1/4 tsp.	1 mL
Salt	1/4 tsp.	1 mL
Lean ground beef	1 lb.	454 g
ORANGE MAYONNAISE		
Mayonnaise	1/2 cup	125 mL
Frozen concentrated orange juice, thawed	1 1/2 tbsp.	25 mL
Hamburger buns, split	4	4

Combine first 14 ingredients in large bowl.

Add ground beef. Mix well. Divide into 4 equal portions. Shape into 4 inch (10 cm) diameter patties. Preheat gas barbecue to medium. (For other cooking methods, see page 8.) Cook patties on greased grill for 5 to 7 minutes per side until fully cooked, and internal temperature of beef reaches 160°F (71°C).

Orange Mayonnaise: Combine mayonnaise and concentrated orange juice in small bowl. Makes about 1/2 cup (125 mL).

Spread each bun with Orange Mayonnaise. Serve patties in buns. Makes 4 burgers.

1 burger: 601 Calories; 36 g Total Fat (18.5 g Mono, 8.7 g Poly, 6.7 g Sat); 74 mg Cholesterol; 41 g Carbohydrate; 2 g Fibre; 27 g Protein; 1210 mg Sodium

Mango Pepper Patties

A colourful and delicious way to dress up ground beef patties.
Be sure to select red peppers that are large enough to make nice rings.

MANGO SALSA

Large red peppers, halved crosswise	2	2
Diced ripe mango	1 cup	250 mL
Thinly sliced green onion	1/4 cup	60 mL
Apple cider vinegar	1 tbsp.	15 mL
Granulated sugar	1 tbsp.	15 mL
Cooking oil	2 tsp.	10 mL
Salt	1/8 tsp.	0.5 mL
Pepper, just a pinch		
Large egg	1	1
Graham cracker crumbs	1/2 cup	125 mL
Finely chopped onion	1/2 cup	125 mL
Chili paste (sambal oelek)	1 tbsp.	15 mL
Salt	1/4 tsp.	1 mL
Lean ground beef	1 lb.	454 g

Mango Salsa: Cut one 1 1/2 inch (3.8 cm) ring from each red pepper half, for a total of 4 rings. Set aside. Finely chop remaining red pepper. Put into medium bowl.

Add next 7 ingredients. Stir. Makes about 2 1/4 cups (550 mL) salsa.

Combine next 5 ingredients in large bowl.

Add ground beef. Mix well. Divide into 4 equal portions. Put 1 portion inside each red pepper ring. Flatten into patties to fill rings. Preheat gas barbecue to medium. (For other cooking methods, see page 8.) Cook patties on greased grill for about 10 minutes per side until fully cooked, and internal temperature of beef reaches 160°F (71°C). Serve with Mango Salsa. Serves 4.

1 serving: 338 Calories; 14.8 g Total Fat (6.7 g Mono, 1.5 g Poly, 4.7 g Sat); 111 mg Cholesterol; 28 g Carbohydrate; 3 g Fibre; 24 g Protein; 372 mg Sodium

Pictured on page 36.

Mushroom Burgers

*Mmm, mushrooms! These tasty, moist burgers
are loaded with them, inside and out.*

Large egg	1	1
Chopped fresh white mushrooms	1/2 cup	125 mL
Fine dry bread crumbs	1/2 cup	125 mL
Grated part-skim mozzarella cheese	1/4 cup	60 mL
Tomato sauce	1/4 cup	60 mL
Dried oregano	1 tsp.	5 mL
Lean ground beef	1 lb.	454 g
Cooking oil	1 tsp.	5 mL
Sliced fresh white mushrooms	1 1/2 cups	375 mL
Lemon juice	2 tsp.	10 mL
Salt	1/4 tsp.	1 mL
Pepper	1/4 tsp.	1 mL
Hamburger buns, split	4	4

Combine first 6 ingredients in large bowl.

Add ground beef. Mix well. Divide into 4 equal portions. Shape into 4 to 5 inch (10 to 12.5 cm) diameter patties. Preheat gas barbecue to medium. (For other cooking methods, see page 8.) Cook patties on greased grill for 5 to 7 minutes per side until fully cooked, and internal temperature of beef reaches 160°F (71°C). Transfer to large plate. Cover to keep warm.

Heat cooking oil in medium frying pan on medium-high. Add second amount of mushrooms. Heat and stir for about 2 minutes until mushrooms start to brown. Reduce heat to medium.

Add next 3 ingredients. Cook for about 5 minutes, stirring often, until mushrooms are browned and liquid is evaporated.

Serve patties, topped with mushrooms, in buns. Makes 4 burgers.

1 burger: 428 Calories; 17.7 g Total Fat (7.8 g Mono, 2 g Poly, 5.9 g Sat); 115 mg Cholesterol; 36 g Carbohydrate; 3 g Fibre; 30 g Protein; 722 mg Sodium

Grilled Tournedos

A patty that's puttin' on the ritz! Wrapped with bacon, capped with mushrooms and served on toast rounds, it's ready for a special occasion.

Texas bread slices	8	8
Large egg, fork-beaten	1	1
Steak sauce	2 tbsp.	30 mL
Dijon mustard (with whole seeds)	2 tbsp.	30 mL
Salt	1/8 tsp.	0.5 mL
Pepper	1/8 tsp.	0.5 mL
Lean ground beef	1 lb.	454 g
Precooked bacon slices	8	8
Hard margarine (or butter)	1 tbsp.	15 mL
Large fresh whole white mushrooms, stems removed	8	8
Dry sherry	2 tbsp.	30 mL
Balsamic vinegar	1 tsp.	5 mL
Hard margarine (or butter), softened	3 tbsp.	50 mL
Chopped fresh parsley (or 1/2 tsp., 2 mL, flakes)	2 tsp.	10 mL
Chopped fresh thyme leaves (or 1/4 tsp., 1 mL, dried)	1 tsp.	5 mL
Pepper, sprinkle		

Using 3 inch (7.5 cm) round cookie cutter, cut out circle from centre of each bread slice. Set bread rounds aside. Process remaining bread into crumbs in blender or food processor. Measure 1/2 cup (125 mL) crumbs into large bowl (see Note).

Add next 5 ingredients. Stir.

Add ground beef. Mix well. Divide into 8 equal portions. Shape into 1 1/4 inch (3 cm) thick patties.

Wrap 1 bacon slice around side of each patty. Secure with wooden picks. Preheat gas barbecue to medium. (For other cooking methods, see page 8.) Cook patties on greased grill for 8 to 10 minutes per side until fully cooked, and internal temperature of beef reaches 160°F (71°C). Transfer to large plate. Cover to keep warm.

(continued on next page)

Burgers & Patties

Melt first amount of margarine in medium frying pan on medium. Add mushrooms. Cook for about 5 minutes, stirring often, until softened.

Add sherry and vinegar. Heat and stir until liquid is evaporated. Remove from heat.

Combine remaining 4 ingredients in small bowl. Spread 1 side of each bread round with margarine mixture. Cook on greased grill, margarine-side down, for about 2 minutes until golden. Turn bread over. Toast opposite side. Serve tournedos, topped with mushrooms, on toast rounds. Serves 4.

1 serving: 665 Calories; 33.2 g Total Fat (17 g Mono, 3.6 g Poly, 9.7 g Sat); 122 mg Cholesterol; 54 g Carbohydrate; 3 g Fibre; 35 g Protein; 1242 mg Sodium

Pictured on page 36.

Note: Freeze the remaining crumbs in an airtight container to use in meatloaf or meatball recipes.

Hickory Patties

Not all patties need to be tucked into a bun! These have a delightfully smoky flavour, making them an excellent choice to serve with potato or macaroni salad, roasted potatoes or baked beans.

Large egg	1	1
Fine dry bread crumbs	1/2 cup	125 mL
Chopped onion	1/4 cup	60 mL
Hickory barbecue sauce	1/4 cup	60 mL
Beef bouillon powder	1 tsp.	5 mL
Pepper	1/8 tsp.	0.5 mL
Lean ground beef	1 lb.	454 g
Cooking oil	2 tsp.	10 mL

Combine first 6 ingredients in medium bowl.

Add ground beef. Mix well. Divide into 4 equal portions. Shape into 4 inch (10 cm) diameter patties.

Heat cooking oil in large frying pan on medium. (For other cooking methods, see page 8.) Add patties. Cook for 5 to 7 minutes per side until fully cooked, and internal temperature of beef reaches 160°F (71°C). Makes 4 patties.

1 patty: 359 Calories; 21.8 g Total Fat (9.7 g Mono, 1.9 g Poly, 7.6 g Sat); 118 mg Cholesterol; 14 g Carbohydrate; 2 g Fibre; 25 g Protein; 498 mg Sodium

Pineapple Salsa Patties

Refreshing fruit salsa is a tasty side for these
sesame-studded patties with a terrific teriyaki taste!

PINEAPPLE GINGER SALSA

Pineapple tidbits, drained	1 cup	250 mL
Diced tomato	1/4 cup	60 mL
Sliced green onion	1/4 cup	60 mL
Chopped fresh cilantro or parsley	1 tbsp.	15 mL
Finely chopped pickled ginger slices, drained	1 tbsp.	15 mL
Apple cider vinegar	1 tbsp.	15 mL
Lime juice	1 tbsp.	15 mL
Brown sugar, packed	2 tsp.	10 mL
Grated lime zest	1 tsp.	5 mL
Ground cumin	1/2 tsp.	2 mL
Dried crushed chilies	1/2 tsp.	2 mL
Large egg	1	1
Crushed sesame rice crackers	1 cup	250 mL
Sliced green onion	3 tbsp.	50 mL
Thick teriyaki basting sauce	2 tbsp.	30 mL
Finely chopped pickled ginger slices, drained	1 tbsp.	15 mL
Garlic clove, minced (or 1/4 tsp., 1 mL, powder)	1	1
Lean ground beef	1 lb.	454 g

Pineapple Ginger Salsa: Combine first 11 ingredients in medium bowl. Cover. Chill for at least 1 hour to blend flavours. Makes about 2 cups (500 mL) salsa.

Combine next 6 ingredients in large bowl.

Add ground beef. Mix well. Divide into 4 equal portions. Shape into 1/2 inch (12 mm) thick oval patties. Preheat gas barbecue to medium. (For other cooking methods, see page 8.) Cook patties on greased grill for about 8 minutes per side until fully cooked, and internal temperature of beef reaches 160°F (71°C). Serve with Pineapple Ginger Salsa. Serves 4.

1 serving: 414 Calories; 23.5 g Total Fat (7.9 g Mono, 3.4 g Poly, 9.6 g Sat); 111 mg Cholesterol; 24 g Carbohydrate; 1 g Fibre; 29 g Protein; 682 mg Sodium

Hot Shot Burgers

Spiced just right! Complement these juicy burgers with
a dollop of guacamole, or add your favourite condiments.

Large egg	1	1
White (or brown) bread slice, processed into crumbs	1	1
Finely chopped onion	1/4 cup	60 mL
Chili powder	2 tbsp.	30 mL
White vinegar	1 1/2 tbsp.	25 mL
Worcestershire sauce	1 tsp/	5 mL
Ground oregano	1/2 – 1 tsp.	2 – 5 mL
Salt	1/2 tsp.	2 mL
Pepper	1/2 tsp.	2 mL
Garlic powder	1/4 tsp.	1 mL
Lean ground beef	1 lb.	454 g
Cooking oil	2 tsp.	10 mL
Hamburger buns, split	4	4

Combine first 10 ingredients in medium bowl.

Add ground beef. Mix well. Divide into 4 equal portions. Shape into 4 inch (10 cm) diameter patties.

Heat cooking oil in large frying pan on medium. (For other cooking methods, see page 8.) Add patties. Cook for 5 to 7 minutes per side until fully cooked, and internal temperature of beef reaches 160°F (71°C).

Serve patties in buns. Makes 4 burgers.

1 burger: 372 Calories; 16.4 g Total Fat (7.3 g Mono, 1.7 g Poly, 5 g Sat); 111 mg Cholesterol; 29 g Carbohydrate; 2 g Fibre; 27 g Protein; 699 mg Sodium

Beef And Vegetable Pie

Rich pastry encloses a filling of creamy beef and vegetables.

Cooking oil	2 tsp.	10 mL
Lean ground beef	1 lb.	454 g
Frozen mixed vegetables	2 cups	500 mL
Can of condensed cream of mushroom soup	10 oz.	284 mL
Beef bouillon powder	1 tsp.	5 mL
Onion powder	1/2 tsp.	2 mL
Pepper	1/4 tsp.	1 mL

Pastry for 2 crust 9 inch (22 cm) pie,
your own or a mix

Heat cooking oil in large frying pan on medium. Add ground beef. Scramble-fry for about 10 minutes until no longer pink. Drain. Transfer to medium bowl. Cool. Add next 5 ingredients. Stir.

Divide pastry into 2 portions, making 1 portion slightly larger than the other. Shape each portion into slightly flattened disc. Roll out larger portion on lightly floured surface to about 1/8 inch (3 mm) thickness. Line 9 inch (22 cm) pie plate. Spoon beef mixture into shell. Roll out smaller portion on lightly floured surface to about 1/8 inch (3 mm) thickness. Dampen edge of shell with water. Cover beef mixture with pastry. Trim and crimp decorative edge to seal. Cut 2 or 3 small vents in top to allow steam to escape. Bake on bottom rack in 400°F (205°C) oven for 15 minutes. Reduce heat to 350°F (175°C). Bake for another 35 to 40 minutes until golden. Let stand on wire rack for 10 minutes before serving. Cuts into 6 wedges.

1 wedge: 436 Calories; 25.6 g Total Fat (11 g Mono, 4.2 g Poly, 8.1 g Sat); 40 mg Cholesterol; 33 g Carbohydrate; 2 g Fibre; 18 g Protein; 830 mg Sodium

Pictured on page 35.

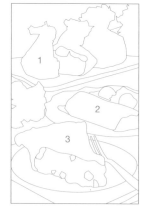

1. Surf 'N' Turf Bundles, page 44
2. Beef And Cheese Rolls, page 42
3. Beef And Vegetable Pie, above

Props courtesy of:
Casa Bugatti
Cherison Enterprises Inc.
The Bay

Lazy Cabbage Roll Casserole

All the flavour, without the fuss! This recipe, from
One-Dish Meals, is perfect for busy cooks who want a taste of tradition.

Bacon slices, diced	4	4
Lean ground beef	1 1/2 lbs.	680 g
Chopped onion	1 cup	250 mL
Tomato juice	1 1/4 cups	300 mL
Can of condensed tomato soup	10 oz.	284 mL
Salt	1/2 tsp.	2 mL
Pepper	1/4 tsp.	1 mL
Coarsely shredded cabbage, lightly packed	8 cups	2 L
Long grain white rice	1/3 cup	75 mL

Cook bacon in large frying pan on medium until crisp. Transfer with slotted spoon to paper towels to drain. Set aside.

Heat 2 tsp. (10 mL) drippings in same pan on medium. Add ground beef and onion. Scramble-fry for about 10 minutes until beef is no longer pink. Drain. Add next 4 ingredients. Stir. Remove from heat.

Spread cabbage evenly in ungreased 9 × 13 inch (22 × 33 cm) pan. Press down lightly. Sprinkle rice over cabbage. Scatter bacon over rice. Spread beef mixture on top. Cover with foil. Bake in 350°F (175°C) oven for about 1 1/2 hours until rice is tender and liquid is absorbed. Serves 6.

1 serving: 316 Calories; 13 g Total Fat (5.5 g Mono, 1.2 g Poly, 4.8 g Sat); 60 mg Cholesterol;
25 g Carbohydrate; 3 g Fibre; 25 g Protein; 885 mg Sodium

1. Grilled Tournedos, page 30
2. Tuscan Stuffed Tomatoes, page 56
3. Mango Pepper Patties, page 28

Props courtesy of:
Danesco Inc.

Creamy Zucchini Wedges

An omelet-like base makes this a great choice for brunch.

Grated zucchini (with peel)	5 cups	1.25 L
Salt	1 tbsp.	15 mL
Grated part-skim mozzarella cheese	3/4 cup	175 mL
Grated sharp Cheddar cheese	1/2 cup	125 mL
Large eggs, fork-beaten	3	3
Cooking oil	2 tsp.	10 mL
Lean ground beef	1 lb.	454 g
Chopped onion	1/2 cup	125 mL
Curry powder	1 tsp.	5 mL
Ground cumin	1/2 tsp.	2 mL
Block of cream cheese, cut up	8 oz.	250 g
Orange juice	3 tbsp.	50 mL
Grated orange zest	1 tsp.	5 mL
Pepper	1/4 tsp.	1 mL
Red medium pepper, cut into 1/4 inch (6 mm) rings	1	1
Grated Parmesan cheese	1/3 cup	75 mL

Put zucchini into large bowl. Sprinkle with salt. Stir. Let stand for 1 hour. Drain. Rinse with cold water. Drain. Gently squeeze out excess water. Return to same bowl.

Add next 3 ingredients. Mix well. Spread evenly in greased 12 inch (30 cm) deep dish pizza pan. Bake in 400°F (205°C) oven for about 20 minutes until set and golden.

Heat cooking oil in large frying pan on medium. Add next 4 ingredients. Scramble-fry for about 10 minutes until ground beef is no longer pink. Remove from heat. Drain.

Add next 4 ingredients. Stir until cream cheese is melted. Spread on top of zucchini crust.

Top with red pepper rings and Parmesan cheese. Bake for 10 to 15 minutes until golden. Cuts into 8 wedges.

1 wedge: 339 Calories; 24.5 g Total Fat (8.2 g Mono, 1.4 g Poly, 13 g Sat); 162 mg Cholesterol; 7 g Carbohydrate; 2 g Fibre; 23 g Protein; 768 mg Sodium

Pictured on page 107.

Saffron Meatball Casserole

Saffron is a little pricey, but its exotic flavour makes this dish a real treat.
Orange zest adds a pleasant taste and aroma.

Large egg	1	1
Finely chopped onion	1/2 cup	125 mL
Crushed buttery crackers	1/2 cup	125 mL
Ground allspice	1 tsp.	5 mL
Salt	1/4 tsp.	1 mL
Cayenne pepper, just a pinch		
Lean ground beef	1 lb.	454 g
Cooking oil	1 tsp.	5 mL
Basmati rice	1 cup	250 mL
Prepared chicken broth	1 1/2 cups	375 mL
Orange juice	1/2 cup	125 mL
Finely chopped green onion	1/4 cup	60 mL
Liquid honey	2 tbsp.	30 mL
Grated orange zest	2 tsp.	10 mL
Saffron threads, crushed (or turmeric)	1/8 tsp.	0.5 mL
Salt	1/8 tsp.	0.5 mL

Combine first 6 ingredients in large bowl.

Add ground beef. Mix well. Roll into 1 1/2 inch (3.8 cm) balls. Arrange on greased baking sheet with sides. Bake in 375°F (190°C) oven for about 20 minutes until fully cooked, and internal temperature of beef reaches 160°F (71°C). Transfer to paper towels to drain. Set aside.

Heat cooking oil in large frying pan on medium. Add rice. Heat and stir for 1 minute.

Add remaining 7 ingredients. Stir. Bring to a boil. Transfer to greased 2 quart (2 L) shallow baking dish. Arrange meatballs in single layer on top of rice mixture. Bake, covered, in 350°F (175°C) oven for about 30 minutes until rice is tender and liquid is absorbed. Serves 4.

1 serving: 510 Calories; 15.7 g Total Fat (6.8 g Mono, 2 g Poly, 5 g Sat); 112 mg Cholesterol; 62 g Carbohydrate; 1 g Fibre; 29 g Protein; 692 mg Sodium

Pictured on page 89.

Phyllo Lasagne

An elegant and impressive dish featuring a fusion of Greek and Italian flavours. Definitely worth the effort!

Ingredient	Imperial	Metric
Cooking oil	2 tsp.	10 mL
Lean ground beef	1 lb.	454 g
Chopped onion	1/2 cup	125 mL
Dried thyme	1 1/2 tsp.	7 mL
Chopped portobello mushrooms	2 cups	500 mL
Cooking oil	1 tsp.	5 mL
Chopped onion	1/2 cup	125 mL
Garlic clove, minced (or 1/4 tsp., 1 mL, powder)	1	1
Cans of artichoke hearts (14 oz., 398 mL, each), drained and chopped	2	2
Roasted red peppers, drained, blotted dry, diced	1/2 cup	125 mL
Dried oregano	1 1/2 tsp.	7 mL
Large eggs	2	2
Grated Asiago cheese	1 cup	250 mL
Goat (chèvre) cheese, softened and cut up	8 oz.	225 g
Sour cream	1/4 cup	60 mL
Pepper	1/2 tsp.	2 mL
Finely chopped walnuts	1/3 cup	75 mL
Fine dry bread crumbs	1/3 cup	75 mL
Frozen phyllo pastry sheets, thawed according to package directions	16	16
Hard margarine (or butter), melted	3/4 cup	175 mL

Heat first amount of cooking oil in large frying pan on medium. Add ground beef, first amount of onion and thyme. Scramble-fry for about 10 minutes until beef is no longer pink. Drain.

Add mushrooms. Cook for 3 to 4 minutes, stirring often, until liquid is evaporated. Transfer to large bowl. Set aside.

Heat second amount of cooking oil in same pan. Add second amount of onion and garlic. Heat and stir for 2 minutes.

(continued on next page)

Add next 3 ingredients. Cook for about 5 minutes, stirring often, until onion is softened. Remove from heat.

Combine next 5 ingredients in medium bowl. Set aside.

Stir walnuts and bread crumbs in small bowl.

Work with pastry sheets 1 at a time. Keep remaining sheets covered with damp tea towel to prevent drying. Lay 1 sheet on work surface. Brush with margarine. Fold in half crosswise. Place in greased 9 x 13 inch (22 x 33 cm) pan. Brush with margarine. Repeat, layering 4 more pastry sheets on top.

To assemble, layer ingredients on top as follows:

1. 1/3 walnut mixture

2. Beef mixture

3. 3 pastry sheets, prepared as above

4. 1/3 walnut mixture

5. Artichoke mixture

6. 3 pastry sheets, prepared as above

7. 1/3 walnut mixture

8. Cheese mixture

9. 5 pastry sheets, prepared as above

Score top layers of pastry by making 2 parallel cuts about 3 inches (7.5 cm) apart across the length of the pan. Cut at an angle across lengthwise cuts to make diamond shapes. Bake, uncovered, in 350°F (175°C) oven for about 45 minutes until crisp and golden. Serves 8.

1 serving: 653 Calories; 44.9 g Total Fat (20 g Mono, 6.5 g Poly, 15.5 g Sat); 122 mg Cholesterol; 36 g Carbohydrate; 3 g Fibre; 29 g Protein; 737 mg Sodium

Pictured on page 108.

Paré Pointer

By rehearsing his sermon, is a minister practising what he preaches?

Beef And Cheese Rolls

Cheesy beef wrapped in golden pastry. Serve these
delicious rolls with a side salad for lunch or dinner.

Cooking oil	2 tsp.	10 mL
Extra-lean ground beef	1 lb.	454 g
Finely chopped onion	1/2 cup	125 mL
Garlic cloves, minced (or 1/2 tsp., 2 mL, powder)	2	2
Pepper	1/4 tsp.	1 mL
Grated havarti cheese	3 cups	750 mL
Crumbled feta cheese	1 cup	250 mL
Dill weed	2 – 3 tsp.	10 – 15 mL
Paprika	1 1/2 tsp.	7 mL
Frozen phyllo pastry sheets, thawed according to package directions	6	6
Hard margarine (or butter), melted	1/4 cup	60 mL
Fine dry bread crumbs	1/4 cup	60 mL
Paprika (optional)	1/2 tsp.	2 mL

Heat cooking oil in large frying pan on medium. Add next 4 ingredients. Scramble-fry for about 10 minutes until ground beef is no longer pink. Drain.

Add next 4 ingredients. Heat and stir until cheese starts to melt. Transfer to large bowl. Let stand until cool enough to handle. On large sheet of waxed paper, roll 1/2 of beef mixture into 16 inch (40 cm) long log. Repeat with remaining beef mixture.

Work with pastry sheets 1 at a time. Keep remaining sheets covered with damp tea towel to prevent drying. Lay 1 sheet lengthwise on work surface. Brush with margarine. Place second sheet on top, aligning edges evenly. Brush with margarine. Place third sheet on top, aligning edges evenly. Sprinkle 1 tbsp. (15 mL) bread crumbs along 1 long side of pastry near edge. Holding waxed paper, carefully place 1 log on top of bread crumbs. Discard waxed paper. Sprinkle 1 tbsp. (15 mL) bread crumbs on top of log. Roll up to enclose. Brush with margarine. Repeat to make second roll. Cut each roll into 4 pieces, for a total of 8 pieces. Arrange, cut-side up, on greased baking sheet with sides.

(continued on next page)

Sprinkle with second amount of paprika. Bake in 375°F (190°C) oven for about 25 minutes until pastry is golden. Serves 4.

1 serving: 421 Calories; 29.2 g Total Fat (11.2 g Mono, 2.2 g Poly, 14 g Sat); 92 mg Cholesterol; 13 g Carbohydrate; trace Fibre; 26 g Protein; 767 mg Sodium

Pictured on page 35.

Beef Corncake

A cheesy crust tops this cornbread-style casserole.

Cooking oil	2 tsp.	10 mL
Lean ground beef	1 lb.	454 g
All-purpose flour	1 cup	250 mL
Yellow cornmeal	1 cup	250 mL
Baking powder	1 tsp.	5 mL
Baking soda	1 tsp.	5 mL
Salt	1 tsp.	5 mL
Large egg	1	1
Cooking oil	1/4 cup	60 mL
Granulated sugar	1 tbsp.	15 mL
Can of cream-style corn	14 oz.	398 mL
Thinly sliced onion	1 1/2 cups	375 mL
Milk	1 cup	250 mL
Seasoned salt, sprinkle		
Grated medium Cheddar cheese	2 cups	500 mL

Heat first amount of cooking oil in large frying pan on medium. Add ground beef. Scramble-fry for about 10 minutes until no longer pink. Remove from heat. Drain. Set aside.

Combine next 5 ingredients in large bowl. Make a well in centre.

Beat next 3 ingredients in medium bowl.

Add beef and next 4 ingredients. Stir. Add to well in cornmeal mixture. Stir until just moistened. Spread evenly in greased 9 x 13 inch (22 x 33 cm) pan.

Sprinkle with cheese. Bake, uncovered, in 350°F (175°C) oven for 45 to 55 minutes until wooden pick inserted in centre comes out clean. Cuts into 8 pieces.

1 piece: 488 Calories; 24.9 g Total Fat (10.4 g Mono, 3.4 g Poly, 9.3 g Sat); 88 mg Cholesterol; 43 g Carbohydrate; 3 g Fibre; 24 g Protein; 897 mg Sodium

Surf 'N' Turf Bundles

Beautiful bundles with the combined flavours of shrimp and beef.

Cooking oil	2 tsp.	10 mL
Lean ground beef	1 lb.	454 g
Chopped fresh white mushrooms	1 cup	250 mL
Finely chopped onion	1/2 cup	125 mL
Can of condensed cream of mushroom soup	10 oz.	284 mL
Fine dry bread crumbs	1 cup	250 mL
Sour cream	1/2 cup	125 mL
Chopped fresh tarragon leaves (or 3/4 tsp., 4 mL, dried)	1 tbsp.	15 mL
Pepper, just a pinch		
Frozen phyllo pastry sheets, thawed according to package directions	12	12
Hard margarine (or butter), melted	1/2 cup	125 mL
Frozen uncooked extra-large shrimp (peeled and deveined), thawed	1 lb.	454 g
Chopped fresh chives (or 3/4 tsp., 4 mL, dried)	1 tbsp.	15 mL

Heat cooking oil in large frying pan on medium. Add ground beef, mushrooms and onion. Scramble-fry for about 10 minutes until beef is no longer pink. Remove from heat. Drain.

Add next 5 ingredients. Stir. Set aside.

Work with pastry sheets 1 at a time. Keep remaining sheets covered with damp tea towel to prevent drying. Lay 1 sheet lengthwise on work surface. Brush with margarine. Place second sheet on top, aligning edges evenly. Brush with margarine. Make 2 crosswise cuts, dividing pastry into 3 equal strips (Diagram 1). Place left and right pastry strips diagonally on centre strip to form an X (Diagram 2).

Diagram 1

Diagram 2

Diagram 3

(continued on next page)

Spoon about 1/2 cup (125 mL) beef mixture onto centre of X. Place 2 or 3 shrimp on top. Sprinkle 1/2 tsp. (2 mL) chives over shrimp. Gather ends of pastry strips and press together at top of filling to enclose, allowing corners to flare outward (Diagram 3). Repeat with remaining ingredients. Place on greased baking sheet with sides. Bake in 350°F (175°C) oven for 20 to 30 minutes until pastry is golden. Makes 6 bundles.

1 bundle: 612 Calories; 34.9 g Total Fat (16.7 g Mono, 6.2 g Poly, 9.4 g Sat); 134 mg Cholesterol; 41 g Carbohydrate; 1 g Fibre; 32 g Protein; 1065 mg Sodium

Pictured on page 35.

Tater Tot Casserole

Tots and teens will want seconds of this easy-to-make casserole, from Jean Paré's Favourites.

Cooking oil	2 tsp.	10 mL
Lean ground beef	1 1/2 lbs.	680 g
Can of condensed cream of celery soup	10 oz.	284 mL
Salt	1 tsp.	5 mL
Pepper	1/4 tsp.	1 mL
Frozen potato tots (gems or puffs)	4 cups	1 L
Water	1/3 cup	75 mL

Heat cooking oil in large frying pan on medium. Add ground beef. Scramble-fry for about 10 minutes until no longer pink. Remove from heat. Drain.

Add 1/2 of soup, salt and pepper. Stir. Spread evenly in ungreased 9 x 9 inch (22 x 22 cm) pan.

Arrange potato tots in single layer on top of beef mixture.

Combine remaining soup and water in small bowl. Drizzle over potato tots. Bake, uncovered, in 350°F (175°C) oven for about 1 hour until potato tots are golden. Serves 6.

1 serving: 378 Calories; 21 g Total Fat (8.7 g Mono, 2.3 g Poly, 8 g Sat); 62 mg Cholesterol; 25 g Carbohydrate; 3 g Fibre; 23 g Protein; 1353 mg Sodium

Variation: Add 2 cups (500 mL) frozen mixed vegetables to beef mixture before spreading in pan. Now you have a full meal!

Leek-Crowned Beef Pie

Before it's cut, this main dish pie looks like a quiche. A rich leek and cheese layer rests atop a savoury beef and sausage combination.

Hard margarine (or butter)	1 tbsp.	15 mL
Medium leeks (white part only), thinly sliced	2	2
Large eggs, fork-beaten	3	3
Homogenized milk	1/2 cup	125 mL
Grated Parmesan cheese	1/4 cup	60 mL
Salt, just a pinch		
Pepper, just a pinch		
Cooking oil	2 tsp.	10 mL
Lean ground beef	1/2 lb.	225 g
Italian sausages, casings removed, chopped	1/2 lb.	225 g
Chopped onion	1 cup	250 mL
Garlic cloves, minced (or 1/2 tsp., 2 mL, powder)	2	2
Can of condensed cream of mushroom soup	10 oz.	284 mL
Dried basil	1/2 tsp.	2 mL
Dried oregano	1/2 tsp.	2 mL
Pastry for 9 inch (22 cm) deep dish pie shell, your own or a mix		

Melt margarine in large frying pan on medium. Add leek. Cook for about 5 minutes, stirring often, until softened. Transfer to medium bowl.

Add next 5 ingredients. Stir. Set aside.

Heat cooking oil in same pan on medium. Add ground beef and sausage. Scramble-fry for about 10 minutes until no longer pink. Transfer with slotted spoon to separate medium bowl. Set aside.

Heat 1 tsp. (5 mL) drippings in same pan on medium. Add onion and garlic. Cook for 5 to 10 minutes, stirring often, until onion is softened.

Add beef mixture and next 3 ingredients. Heat and stir for 1 minute. Cool slightly.

(continued on next page)

Roll out pastry on lightly floured surface to about 1/8 inch (3 mm) thickness. Line 9 inch (22 cm) deep dish pie plate. Trim pastry, leaving 1/2 inch (12 mm) overhang. Roll under and crimp decorative edge. Spread beef mixture evenly in shell. Pour leek mixture over top. Bake on bottom rack in 400°F (205°C) oven for 15 minutes. Reduce heat to 350°F (175°C). Bake for another 35 to 40 minutes until knife inserted in centre comes out clean. Cuts into 6 wedges.

1 wedge: 420 Calories; 27.3 g Total Fat (11.5 g Mono, 4.5 g Poly, 9 g Sat); 149 mg Cholesterol; 25 g Carbohydrate; 2 g Fibre; 19 g Protein; 877 mg Sodium

Pictured on page 53 and on back cover.

 Hot peppers get their fiery heat from the capsaicin contained in their seeds and ribs. Removing the seeds and ribs will reduce the heat. When handling hot peppers, wear rubber gloves and avoid touching your eyes. Remember to wash your hands well afterwards.

Paré Pointer

Why is traffic slowest during rush hour?

Shepherd's Pie

You'll hook them for sure with this steaming
shepherd's pie! First published in Lunches, it's still a hit!

Company's Coming Classic

Cooking oil	2 tsp.	10 mL
Lean ground beef	1 1/2 lbs.	680 g
Chopped onion	1 cup	250 mL
All-purpose flour	1 tbsp.	15 mL
Salt	1 1/2 tsp.	7 mL
Pepper	1/4 tsp.	1 mL
Milk	1/3 cup	75 mL
Cooked peas	1 cup	250 mL
Cooked sliced carrot	1 cup	250 mL
Ketchup	1 tbsp.	15 mL
Worcestershire sauce	1 tsp.	5 mL
Prepared horseradish	1 tsp.	5 mL
Potatoes, peeled, cut up	1 1/2 lbs.	680 g
Water		
Milk	3 – 4 tbsp.	50 – 60 mL
Hard margarine (or butter)	1 tbsp.	15 mL
Seasoned salt	1/2 tsp.	2 mL
Hard margarine (or butter), melted	2 tbsp.	30 mL
Paprika, sprinkle		

Heat cooking oil in large frying pan on medium. Add ground beef and onion. Scramble-fry for about 10 minutes until beef is no longer pink. Drain.

Add flour, salt and pepper. Stir well. Slowly add first amount of milk, stirring constantly. Heat and stir for about 2 minutes until boiling and thickened. Add next 5 ingredients. Stir. Spread evenly in greased 8 x 8 inch (20 x 20 cm) pan. Set aside.

Cook potato in water in large saucepan until tender. Drain. Add second amount of milk, first amount of margarine and seasoned salt. Mash. Spread on top of beef mixture.

Brush mashed potatoes with second amount of margarine. Using fork, score wave pattern on top. Sprinkle with paprika. Bake, uncovered, in 350°F (175°C) oven for about 30 minutes until heated through and mashed potatoes are golden. Serves 6.

1 serving: 369 Calories; 17.6 g Total Fat (9 g Mono, 1.5 g Poly, 5.3 g Sat); 58 mg Cholesterol; 28 g Carbohydrate; 4 g Fibre; 25 g Protein; 918 mg Sodium

Greek Salad Pizza

Colourful, Greek-style toppings on a knife-and-fork pizza. Serve with lemon wedges to squeeze over top for an extra splash of flavour.

Cooking oil	1 tsp.	5 mL
Lean ground beef	1/2 lb.	225 g
Chopped onion	1/2 cup	125 mL
Garlic clove, minced (or 1/4 tsp., 1 mL, powder)	1	1
Box of frozen chopped spinach, thawed and squeezed dry	10 oz.	300 g
Dried oregano	1 tsp.	5 mL
Prebaked pizza crust (12 inch, 30 cm, diameter)	1	1
Pizza sauce	1/4 cup	60 mL
Grated part-skim mozzarella cheese	1 cup	250 mL
Can of sliced ripe olives, drained	4 1/2 oz.	125 mL
Crumbled feta cheese	1 cup	250 mL
Chopped tomato	1 cup	250 mL
Chopped fresh mint leaves (optional)	1 tbsp.	15 mL

Heat cooking oil in medium frying pan on medium. Add ground beef, onion and garlic. Scramble-fry for about 10 minutes until beef is no longer pink. Drain.

Add spinach and oregano. Heat and stir for 2 minutes.

Place pizza crust on ungreased baking sheet. Spread pizza sauce on crust. Scatter beef mixture over sauce.

Sprinkle with mozzarella cheese. Bake in 450°F (230°C) oven for about 10 minutes until crust is golden and cheese is melted and starting to brown.

Scatter remaining 4 ingredients, in order given, over top. Cuts into 8 wedges.

1 wedge: 258 Calories; 12 g Total Fat (3.7 g Mono, 0.7 g Poly, 5.7 g Sat); 42 mg Cholesterol; 22 g Carbohydrate; 2 g Fibre; 16 g Protein; 590 mg Sodium

Pictured on page 108.

Picadillo Pie

Picadillo (pee-kah-DEE-yoh) is a meat hash often made with ground beef.
The inclusion of fruit makes it distinct. Picadillo is traditionally used as
a filling in various dishes—here it forms the base of a tasty casserole.

Cooking oil	2 tsp.	10 mL
Lean ground beef	1 1/2 lbs.	680 g
Chopped fresh white mushrooms	1 cup	250 mL
Chopped onion	1 cup	250 mL
Garlic cloves, minced (or 1/2 tsp., 2 mL, powder)	2	2
Chili powder	2 tsp.	10 mL
Ground cumin	1 tsp.	5 mL
Dried oregano	1 tsp.	5 mL
Can of diced tomatoes (with juice)	28 oz.	796 mL
Sliced pimiento-stuffed olives	3/4 cup	175 mL
Chopped dried apricot	1/2 cup	125 mL
Dark raisins	1/2 cup	125 mL
Sweet potatoes (or yams), peeled, cut up	2 lbs.	900 g
Potatoes, peeled, cut up	1 lb.	454 g
Water		
Hard margarine (or butter)	3 tbsp.	50 mL
Yellow cornmeal	3 tbsp.	50 mL
Large egg, fork-beaten	1	1
Dried oregano	1/2 tsp.	2 mL
Salt	1/4 tsp.	1 mL
Pepper	1/4 tsp.	1 mL

Heat cooking oil in large frying pan on medium. Add ground beef. Scramble-fry for about 10 minutes until no longer pink. Drain.

Add next 6 ingredients. Cook for about 5 to 10 minutes, stirring occasionally, until onion is softened and liquid is evaporated.

Add next 4 ingredients. Stir. Bring to a boil. Spread evenly in greased 3 quart (3 L) shallow baking dish. Set aside.

Cook sweet potato and potato in water in large saucepan until tender. Drain.

(continued on next page)

Add remaining 6 ingredients. Mash. Spread on top of beef mixture. Using fork, score decorative pattern on potato mixture. Bake, uncovered, in 375°F (190°C) oven for about 40 minutes until potato mixture is firm. Cuts into 8 pieces.

1 piece: 417 Calories; 16.2 g Total Fat (8.4 g Mono, 1.6 g Poly, 4.4 g Sat); 69 mg Cholesterol; 50 g Carbohydrate; 6 g Fibre; 21 g Protein; 714 mg Sodium

Pictured on page 54.

Baked Spinach Portobellos

Basil and assertive, salty cheeses make these a delightful treat.

Bacon slices, diced	4	4
Lean ground beef	1/2 lb.	225 g
Chopped onion	1/2 cup	125 mL
Garlic clove, minced (or 1/4 tsp., 1 mL, powder)	1	1
Box of frozen chopped spinach, thawed and squeezed dry	10 oz.	300 g
Chopped fresh basil (or 3/4 tsp., 4 mL, dried)	1 tbsp.	15 mL
Ground nutmeg	1/4 tsp.	1 mL
Goat (chévre) cheese, cut up	4 oz.	113 g
Crumbled feta cheese	3/4 cup	175 mL
Portobello mushrooms (about 4 inch, 10 cm, diameter)	6	6

Cook bacon in large frying pan on medium until almost crisp. Add ground beef, onion and garlic. Scramble-fry for about 10 minutes until beef is no longer pink. Drain.

Add spinach, basil and nutmeg. Heat and stir for about 2 minutes until spinach is heated through and basil is fragrant. Add goat and feta cheeses. Stir. Remove from heat.

Remove stems from mushrooms. Using small spoon, remove gills from mushroom caps. Spoon beef mixture into mushrooms. Arrange in ungreased 9 x 13 inch (22 x 33 cm) pan. Cover with foil. Bake in 375°F (190°C) oven for about 30 minutes until mushrooms are softened. Remove foil. Bake for another 10 minutes until top of beef mixture is firm and slightly crisp. Makes 6 stuffed mushrooms.

1 stuffed mushroom: 234 Calories; 14.3 g Total Fat (4.2 g Mono, 0.9 g Poly, 7.9 g Sat); 52 mg Cholesterol; 11 g Carbohydrate; 3 g Fibre; 18 g Protein; 406 mg Sodium

Hot Tamale Two-Step

Warm things up with our spicy twist on the tamale pie.

Cooking oil	2 tsp.	10 mL
Lean ground beef	1 lb.	454 g
Chili powder	1 tbsp.	15 mL
Seasoned salt	2 tsp.	10 mL
Garlic powder	1/2 tsp.	2 mL
Onion powder	1/2 tsp.	2 mL
Large eggs	2	2
Milk	2 cups	500 mL
Frozen kernel corn	2 cups	500 mL
Can of diced tomatoes (with juice)	14 oz.	398 mL
Yellow cornmeal	1 cup	250 mL
Can of sliced jalapeño peppers, drained	4 oz.	114 mL
Grated sharp Cheddar cheese	1 cup	250 mL
Can of sliced ripe olives, drained	4 1/2 oz.	125 mL

Heat cooking oil in large frying pan on medium. Add ground beef. Scramble-fry for about 10 minutes until no longer pink. Drain. Add next 4 ingredients. Heat and stir for about 1 minute until fragrant. Remove from heat.

Combine next 6 ingredients in large bowl. Add beef mixture. Stir well. Spread evenly in greased 2 quart (2 L) casserole. Bake, uncovered, in 375°F (175°C) oven for about 1 hour until firm.

Sprinkle with cheese and olives. Bake for another 5 to 10 minutes until cheese is melted. Serves 6.

1 serving: 442 Calories; 19.2 g Total Fat (7.4 g Mono, 1.7 g Poly, 8.2 g Sat); 134 mg Cholesterol; 41 g Carbohydrate; 4 g Fibre; 28 g Protein; 811 mg Sodium

Pictured on page 54.

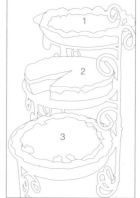

1. Leek-Crowned Beef Pie, page 46
2. Ricotta Swiss Wedges, page 97
3. Cheeseburger Pie, page 58

Props courtesy of: Casa Bugatti
Cherison Enterprises Inc.
Pyrex® Bakeware

Beefy Burrito Bake

Tangy cheese makes these stuffed tortillas especially tempting.

Cooking oil	2 tsp.	10 mL
Lean ground beef	1 lb.	454 g
Sliced fresh white mushrooms	1 1/2 cups	375 mL
Chopped onion	1/2 cup	125 mL
Low-sodium prepared beef broth	1 1/4 cups	300 mL
Envelope of reduced sodium taco seasoning mix	1 1/4 oz.	35 g
Flour tortillas (9 inch, 22 cm, diameter)	8	8
Skim evaporated milk	1 cup	250 mL
Pasteurized cheese loaf, cubed	9 oz.	250 g

Heat cooking oil in large frying pan on medium. Add ground beef, mushrooms and onion. Scramble-fry for about 10 minutes until beef is no longer pink. Drain. Add broth and taco seasoning. Stir. Bring to a boil. Reduce heat to medium-low. Simmer, uncovered, for about 10 minutes until thickened.

Spoon about 1/4 cup (60 mL) beef mixture along centre of each tortilla. Fold sides over filling. Roll up from bottom to enclose. Arrange, seam-side down, on greased baking sheet with sides. Bake in 350°F (175°C) oven for about 15 minutes until heated through.

Heat and stir evaporated milk and cheese in medium saucepan on medium for about 10 minutes until cheese is melted. Spoon over burritos. Serves 8.

1 serving: 398 Calories; 19.2 g Total Fat (6.8 g Mono, 2 g Poly, 8.7 g Sat); 59 mg Cholesterol; 32 g Carbohydrate; 2 g Fibre; 24 g Protein; 1193 mg Sodium

1. Picadillo Pie, page 50
2. Hot Tamale Two-Step, page 52
3. Fiesta Strata, page 65

Props courtesy of: Anchor Hocking Canada
Danesco Inc.
Out of the Fire Studio
Pyrex® Bakeware

Tuscan Stuffed Tomatoes

You can almost feel the warmth of the Tuscan sun when you
feast your eyes on these golden-topped, stuffed tomatoes.
Add a salad and a glass of wine—Buon Appetito!

Large tomatoes	8	8
Salt, sprinkle		
Cooking oil	1 tsp.	5 mL
Lean ground beef	1 lb.	454 g
Finely chopped green onion	1/2 cup	125 mL
Garlic clove, minced (or 1/4 tsp., 1 mL, powder)	1	1
Salt	1/4 tsp.	1 mL
Pepper	1/8 tsp.	0.5 mL
Cooked orzo (about 1/2 cup, 125 mL, uncooked)	1 cup	250 mL
Chopped fresh parsley (or 1 tbsp., 15 mL, flakes)	1/4 cup	60 mL
Coarsely chopped pine nuts, toasted (see Tip, page 129)	3 tbsp.	50 mL
Dried oregano	1 tbsp.	15 mL
Dried crushed chilies	1/2 tsp.	2 mL
Salt	1/2 tsp.	2 mL
Crumbled feta cheese	1/2 cup	125 mL
Grated Parmesan cheese	1/4 cup	60 mL
Grated Parmesan cheese	1/4 cup	60 mL
Chopped green onion	1/4 cup	60 mL
Kalamata olives, pitted (see Note)	8	8

Trim 1/4 inch (6 mm) slice from bottom of each tomato. Using small spoon, scoop out pulp from each tomato, reserving 1 cup (250 mL). Sprinkle inside of each with salt. Place cut-side down, on 2 large microwave-safe plates. Microwave each plate on high (100%) for about 1 minute until tomatoes are slightly softened. Set aside.

Heat cooking oil in large frying pan on medium. Add next 5 ingredients. Scramble-fry for about 10 minutes until ground beef is no longer pink. Drain.

(continued on next page)

Add reserved tomato pulp and next 6 ingredients. Stir. Cook for 5 minutes, stirring occasionally.

Add feta cheese and first amount of Parmesan cheese. Stir. Remove from heat. Arrange tomatoes on greased baking sheet with sides. Fill with beef mixture.

Sprinkle with second amounts of Parmesan cheese and onion. Top with olives. Broil on centre rack in oven for 8 to 10 minutes until Parmesan cheese is golden. Makes 8 stuffed tomatoes.

1 stuffed tomato: 268 Calories; 12.7 g Total Fat (4.6 g Mono, 1.6 g Poly, 5.2 g Sat); 44 mg Cholesterol; 21 g Carbohydrate; 3 g Fibre; 19 g Protein; 539 mg Sodium

Pictured on page 36.

Note: To pit an olive, place it on a cutting board and press the olive with the flat side of a wide knife until you feel the olive give. The flesh will split, making it easy to remove the pit. Alternatively, use a sharp knife to split the olive from top to bottom, cutting through the flesh to the pit.

Paré Pointer

The turtles crossed the road to get to the shell station.

Cheeseburger Pie

*The whole family will love this hearty meal. You can also
cut the dough into biscuits to serve with soup or chili.*

Cooking oil	2 tsp.	10 mL
Lean ground beef	1 lb.	454 g
Chopped onion	1/2 cup	125 mL
Ketchup	2 tbsp.	30 mL
Salt	3/4 tsp.	4 mL
Pepper	1/4 tsp.	1 mL
BISCUIT CRUST		
All-purpose flour	2 cups	500 mL
Baking powder	1 tbsp.	15 mL
Granulated sugar	2 tsp.	10 mL
Salt	1/2 tsp.	2 mL
Milk	2/3 cup	150 mL
Cooking oil	1/3 cup	75 mL
Can of diced tomatoes, drained	14 oz.	398 mL
Granulated sugar	1/2 tsp.	2 mL
Grated medium Cheddar cheese	1 cup	250 mL

Heat cooking oil in large frying pan on medium. Add ground beef and
onion. Scramble-fry for about 10 minutes until beef is no longer pink.
Drain.

Add next 3 ingredients. Stir. Cool.

Biscuit Crust: Combine first 4 ingredients in large bowl. Make a well
in centre.

Add milk and cooking oil to well. Stir until just moistened. Roll into ball.
Press into bottom and up side of greased 9 inch (22 cm) pie plate. Spread
beef mixture evenly in crust.

Combine tomatoes and second amount of sugar in small bowl. Spoon over
beef mixture. Sprinkle with cheese. Bake in 350°F (175°C) oven for about
45 minutes until crust is golden and cheese is melted. Cuts into 6 wedges.

*1 wedge: 525 Calories; 28.1 g Total Fat (13.2 g Mono, 4.9 g Poly, 8 g Sat); 61 mg Cholesterol;
43 g Carbohydrate; 2 g Fibre; 25 g Protein; 1017 mg Sodium*

Pictured on page 53 and on back cover.

Hash Brown Pizza

*The enticing aroma of this recipe, from
Jean Paré's Favourites, will call everyone to
the kitchen for dinner so you don't have to.*

Large egg	1	1
Can of condensed Cheddar cheese soup	10 oz.	284 mL
Pepper	1/2 tsp.	2 mL
Bag of frozen hash brown potatoes, thawed	2 1/4 lbs.	1 kg
Cooking oil	2 tsp.	10 mL
Lean ground beef	1 lb.	454 g
Finely chopped onion	2 tbsp.	30 mL
All-purpose flour	2 tbsp.	30 mL
Can of condensed tomato soup	10 oz.	284 mL
Granulated sugar	2 tsp.	10 mL
Garlic powder	1/4 tsp.	1 mL
Salt	1/2 tsp.	2 mL
Pepper	1/8 tsp.	0.5 mL
Grated medium Cheddar cheese	2 cups	500 mL

Combine first 3 ingredients in large bowl. Add hash brown potatoes. Stir
well. Spread evenly in greased 12 inch (30 cm) pizza pan, pressing with
back of spoon to form rim around edge. Bake in 450°F (230°C) oven for
20 to 25 minutes until firm.

Heat cooking oil in large frying pan on medium. Add ground beef and
onion. Scramble-fry for about 10 minutes until beef is no longer pink.
Drain.

Add flour. Stir well. Add next 5 ingredients. Heat and stir for about
5 minutes until boiling and thickened. Remove from heat.

Sprinkle 1/2 of cheese over potato crust. Spread beef mixture on top of
cheese. Sprinkle with remaining cheese. Bake for 4 to 5 minutes until
cheese is melted and bubbling. Cuts into 8 wedges.

*1 wedge: 414 Calories; 21.1 g Total Fat (6.9 g Mono, 1.6 g Poly, 10.8 g Sat); 96 mg Cholesterol;
34 g Carbohydrate; 3 g Fibre; 23 g Protein; 948 mg Sodium*

Beef Barley Cabbage Rolls

Cabbage roll fans are sure to be impressed with these large, hearty rolls!
Wholesome barley makes these just a little different.

Large head of green cabbage	1	1
Boiling water		
Low-sodium prepared beef broth	3 cups	750 mL
Pearl barley	1 cup	250 mL
Bacon slices, cooked crisp and crumbled	8	8
Medium onion, finely chopped	1	1
Large carrot, finely chopped	1	1
Large celery rib, finely chopped	1	1
Chopped fresh thyme leaves	2 tsp.	10 mL
(or 1/2 tsp., 2 mL, dried)		
Salt	1/4 tsp.	1 mL
Pepper	1/8 tsp.	0.5 mL
Ground cloves	1/8 tsp.	0.5 mL
Lean ground beef	2 lbs.	900 g
Tomato juice	1 1/4 cups	300 mL
Low-sodium prepared beef broth	1 cup	250 mL
Low-sodium prepared beef broth, approximately	1 2/3 cups	400 mL
Hard margarine (or butter)	1 1/2 tbsp.	25 mL
All-purpose flour	3 tbsp.	50 mL
Drops of liquid gravy browner (optional)	1 – 2	1 – 2

Remove core from cabbage. Trim about 1/2 inch (12 mm) slice from bottom. Place, cut-side down, in Dutch oven. Cover with boiling water. Cover Dutch oven with foil. Heat on medium-low for about 30 minutes, using tongs to remove leaves to tea towel as they start to soften and loosen. Blot dry. Cut 'V' shape along tough ribs of leaves to remove. Cut larger leaves into 2 equal pieces. Set aside.

Measure first amount of broth into large saucepan. Bring to a boil on high. Add barley. Stir. Return to a boil. Reduce heat to medium-low. Simmer, covered, for about 20 minutes, stirring occasionally, until tender and broth is absorbed. Cool.

(continued on next page)

Combine next 8 ingredients in large bowl.

Add barley and ground beef. Mix well. Spoon about 1/2 cup (125 mL) beef mixture onto centre of 1 cabbage leaf. Fold sides over filling. Roll up tightly from bottom to enclose. Repeat with remaining cabbage leaves and beef mixture. Arrange cabbage rolls tightly together, seam-side down, in single layer in greased large roasting pan. Layer any extra cabbage leaves on top of rolls.

Combine tomato juice and second amount of broth in small bowl. Pour over cabbage rolls. Bake, covered, in 350°F (175°C) oven for about 2 hours until cabbage is softened. Carefully spoon liquid from roasting pan into 4 cup (1 L) heatproof liquid measure. Cover cabbage rolls to keep warm.

Add enough of third amount of broth to liquid measure to equal 3 cups (750 mL) liquid.

Melt margarine in medium saucepan on medium. Add flour. Heat and stir for about 2 minutes until golden. Slowly add broth mixture, stirring constantly. Bring to a boil. Reduce heat to medium-low. Simmer, uncovered, for about 20 minutes, stirring often, until thickened.

Add gravy browner. Stir. Pour over cabbage rolls. Serves 8.

1 serving: 460 Calories; 23.1 g Total Fat (10.4 g Mono, 1.6 g Poly, 8.5 g Sat); 69 mg Cholesterol; 34 g Carbohydrate; 5 g Fibre; 30 g Protein; 933 mg Sodium

Meaty Lasagne

A classic lasagne at first glance, but with a
touch of fennel for a subtle, tasty difference.

Cooking oil	2 tsp.	10 mL
Lean ground beef	2 lbs.	900 g
Tomato pasta sauce	3 cups	750 mL
Finely chopped onion	2 tbsp.	30 mL
Worcestershire sauce	1 tsp.	5 mL
Dried oregano	1 tsp.	5 mL
Fennel seed	1/2 tsp.	2 mL
Pepper	1/4 tsp.	1 mL
Large eggs	2	2
Ricotta cheese	3 cups	750 mL
Grated Parmesan cheese	1/3 cup	75 mL
Ground nutmeg	1/8 tsp.	0.5 mL
Lasagna noodles	12	12
Grated part-skim mozzarella cheese	3 cups	750 mL
Grated Parmesan cheese	1/2 cup	125 mL

Heat cooking oil in large deep frying pan or Dutch oven on medium. Add ground beef. Scramble-fry for about 10 minutes until no longer pink. Drain.

Add next 6 ingredients. Stir. Bring to a boil. Reduce heat to medium-low. Simmer, covered, for 25 minutes, stirring occasionally. Remove from heat. Set aside.

Combine next 4 ingredients in medium bowl. Set aside.

Cook noodles in boiling salted water in large uncovered pot or Dutch oven for 12 to 15 minutes, stirring occasionally, until tender but firm. Drain. Rinse with cold water. Drain well.

(continued on next page)

To assemble, layer ingredients in greased 9 × 13 inch (22 × 33 cm) pan as follows:

1. 4 lasagna noodles, slightly overlapping to fit pan

2. 1/3 ricotta cheese mixture

3. 1/3 meat sauce

4. 4 lasagna noodles, slightly overlapping

5. 1/3 ricotta cheese mixture

6. 1/3 meat sauce

7. 4 lasagna noodles, slightly overlapping

8. 1/3 ricotta cheese mixture

9. 1/3 meat sauce

Sprinkle with mozzarella cheese and second amount of Parmesan cheese. Bake, uncovered, in 350°F (175°C) oven for about 45 minutes until heated through and cheese is melted and golden. Serves 12.

1 serving: 503 Calories; 26.9 g Total Fat (9.5 g Mono, 2 g Poly, 13.3 g Sat); 130 mg Cholesterol; 28 g Carbohydrate; 1 g Fibre; 36 g Protein; 695 mg Sodium

Paré Pointer

It's hard to find something you've lost—except for those few pounds.

Porcupine Stew

In this tasty slow-cooker recipe, old-fashioned meatballs bristle with rice.

Medium onion, cut into 8 wedges	1	1
Coarsely chopped carrot	4 cups	1 L
Red baby potatoes, larger ones cut in half	1 lb.	454 g
Dill weed	1 tsp.	5 mL
Pepper, sprinkle		
Large egg	1	1
Long grain white rice	1/2 cup	125 mL
Finely chopped onion	1/3 cup	75 mL
Fine dry bread crumbs	1/4 cup	60 mL
Garlic cloves, minced (or 1/2 tsp., 2 mL, powder)	2	2
Worcestershire sauce	2 tsp.	10 mL
Seasoned salt	1/2 tsp.	2 mL
Pepper	1/4 tsp.	1 mL
Lean ground beef	1 1/2 lbs.	680 g
Cooking oil	2 tsp.	10 mL
Can of condensed tomato soup	10 oz.	284 mL
Prepared beef broth	1 cup	250 mL
Water	1/2 cup	125 mL

Layer onion wedges, carrot and potatoes, in order given, in 4 to 5 quart (4 to 5 L) slow cooker. Sprinkle with dill weed and first amount of pepper.

Combine next 8 ingredients in large bowl.

Add ground beef. Mix well. Divide into 12 equal portions. Roll into balls.

Heat cooking oil in large frying pan on medium. Add meatballs. Cook for about 10 minutes, turning often, until fully cooked and internal temperature of beef reaches 160°F (71°C). Arrange meatballs in single layer on top of potatoes.

Combine remaining 3 ingredients in small bowl. Pour over meatballs. Cover. Cook on Low for 8 to 10 hours or on High for 4 to 5 hours. Remove meatballs and vegetables with slotted spoon to separate large serving bowls. Top with sauce from slow cooker, or serve on the side. Serves 6.

(continued on next page)

1 serving: 505 Calories; 21 g Total Fat (9 g Mono, 1.9 g Poly, 7.5 g Sat); 100 mg Cholesterol; 50 g Carbohydrate; 6 g Fibre; 29 g Protein; 813 mg Sodium

Pictured on page 144.

Fiesta Strata

This make-ahead Tex-Mex dish needs to be chilled overnight before baking. Serve with salad and salsa, and let the fiesta begin!

Cooking oil	2 tsp.	10 mL
Lean ground beef	1 lb.	454 g
Chopped onion	1/2 cup	125 mL
Roasted red peppers, drained, blotted dry, cut into strips	1/2 cup	125 mL
Can of diced green chilies	4 oz.	113 g
Chili powder	1/2 tsp.	2 mL
Flour tortillas (9 inch, 22 cm, diameter)	6	6
Large eggs	4	4
Milk	2 cups	500 mL
Ground cumin	1/4 tsp.	1 mL
Grated Monterey Jack cheese	1 1/2 cups	375 mL

Heat cooking oil in large frying pan on medium. Add ground beef and onion. Scramble-fry for about 10 minutes until beef is no longer pink. Drain.

Add next 3 ingredients. Heat and stir for 2 to 3 minutes until fragrant. Remove from heat.

Place 1 tortilla in greased 3 quart (3 L) round casserole. Fold edge if necessary to fit into casserole. Spread about 1/2 cup (125 mL) beef mixture on top. Repeat, layering remaining tortillas and beef mixture, ending with a tortilla.

Beat next 3 ingredients with whisk in medium bowl. Pour over top.

Sprinkle with cheese. Cover. Chill overnight to allow flavours to blend and tortillas to absorb liquid. Bake, uncovered, in 350°F (175°C) oven for about 1 1/4 hours until puffed and golden. Cuts into 8 wedges.

1 wedge: 360 Calories; 18.3 g Total Fat (6.8 g Mono, 2 g Poly, 7.8 g Sat); 159 mg Cholesterol; 24 g Carbohydrate; 2 g Fibre; 24 g Protein; 366 mg Sodium

Pictured on page 54.

Sloppy Ginos

Italian-style sloppy joes. This zesty chili is served on focaccia bread instead of buns. A hearty knife-and-fork sandwich.

Cooking oil	2 tsp.	10 mL
Lean ground beef	1/2 lb.	225 g
Italian sausages, casings removed, chopped	1/2 lb.	225 g
Chopped onion	1/2 cup	125 mL
Garlic clove, minced (or 1/4 tsp., 1 mL, powder)	1	1
Diced green pepper	1/4 cup	60 mL
Diced red pepper	1/4 cup	60 mL
Italian seasoning	1/2 tsp.	2 mL
Fennel seed	1/4 tsp.	1 mL
Dried crushed chilies	1/4 tsp.	1 mL
Can of tomato sauce	14 oz.	398 mL
Herb focaccia bread (10 inch, 25 cm, diameter)	1	1

Heat cooking oil in large frying pan on medium. Add next 4 ingredients. Scramble-fry for about 10 minutes until ground beef and sausage are no longer pink. Drain.

Add next 5 ingredients. Stir. Cook for about 5 minutes, stirring occasionally, until green and red peppers are tender.

Add tomato sauce. Heat and stir for about 1 minute until heated through.

Cut bread into 6 wedges. Place on ungreased baking sheet. Broil on top rack in oven for about 2 minutes until golden. Remove to dinner plates. Top with beef mixture. Serves 6.

1 serving: 339 Calories; 12.7 g Total Fat (6.1 g Mono, 2.2 g Poly, 3.2 g Sat); 33 mg Cholesterol; 40 g Carbohydrate; 3 g Fibre; 16 g Protein; 1012 mg Sodium

Paré Pointer

We were given a mouth that closes and ears that do not—there's a message here.

Chilies & Sauces

Meat Sauce

This versatile sauce, from The Beef Book,
is just the thing over spaghetti or in a lasagne.
The chili heat can be adjusted, depending on personal preference.

Cooking oil	2 tsp.	10 mL
Lean ground beef	1 lb.	454 g
Medium onions, chopped	2	2
Celery ribs, chopped	2	2
Green medium pepper, chopped	1	1
Garlic clove, minced (or 1/4 tsp., 1 mL, powder)	1	1
Can of diced tomatoes (with juice)	28 oz.	796 mL
Can of crushed tomatoes	14 oz.	398 mL
Water	1/3 cup	75 mL
Chopped fresh parsley (or 2 1/2 tsp., 12 mL, flakes)	3 tbsp.	50 mL
Chopped fresh basil (or 3/4 tsp., 4 mL, dried)	1 tbsp.	15 mL
Bay leaf	1	1
Dried oregano	1 tsp.	5 mL
Dried crushed chilies	1 tsp.	5 mL
Granulated sugar	1/2 tsp.	2 mL
Salt	1/2 tsp.	2 mL
Pepper, sprinkle		

Heat cooking oil in large saucepan on medium. Add next 5 ingredients. Scramble-fry for about 10 minutes until ground beef is no longer pink. Drain.

Add remaining 11 ingredients. Stir. Bring to a boil. Reduce heat to medium-low. Simmer, uncovered, for about 45 minutes, stirring occasionally, until vegetables are softened and sauce is thickened. Discard bay leaf. Serves 6.

1 serving: 196 Calories; 8.5 g Total Fat (3.8 g Mono, 1 g Poly, 2.7 g Sat); 39 mg Cholesterol;
15 g Carbohydrate; 3 g Fibre; 16 g Protein; 574 mg Sodium

Tandoori Chili

Excellent flavour and fiery heat in a complex
spice combination. Serve with pappadums.

Cooking oil	2 tsp.	10 mL
Lean ground beef	1 lb.	454 g
Chopped onion	1 cup	250 mL
Finely grated, peeled gingerroot	1 tbsp.	15 mL
(or 3/4 tsp., 4 mL, ground ginger)		
Garlic clove, minced (or 1/4 tsp., 1 mL,	1	1
powder)		
Paprika	3 tbsp.	50 mL
Dried crushed chilies	2 tsp.	10 mL
Ground cumin	1 1/2 tsp.	7 mL
Ground cardamom	1/2 tsp.	2 mL
Ground coriander	1/2 tsp.	2 mL
Salt	1/2 tsp.	2 mL
Pepper	1/2 tsp.	2 mL
Ground cloves	1/4 tsp.	1 mL
Ground cinnamon	1/4 tsp.	1 mL
Can of chickpeas (garbanzo beans),	19 oz.	540 mL
rinsed and drained		
Can of diced tomatoes (with juice)	14 oz.	398 mL
Water	1 cup	250 mL
Can of tomato sauce	7 1/2 oz.	213 mL
Plain yogurt	1 cup	250 mL

Heat cooking oil in large frying pan or Dutch oven on medium. Add next 4 ingredients. Scramble-fry for about 10 minutes until ground beef is no longer pink. Drain.

Add next 9 ingredients. Heat and stir for about 1 minute until fragrant.

Add next 4 ingredients. Stir. Bring to a boil. Reduce heat to medium-low. Simmer, uncovered, for about 20 minutes, stirring occasionally, until slightly thickened.

Add yogurt. Heat and stir for about 10 minutes until heated through. Serves 6.

1 serving: 274 Calories; 10.7 g Total Fat (4.3 g Mono, 1.6 g Poly, 3.3 g Sat); 40 mg Cholesterol; 25 g Carbohydrate; 4 g Fibre; 21 g Protein; 706 mg Sodium

Pictured on page 72.

Chilies & Sauces

Rosy Beef Sauce

A creamy sauce brimming with vegetables. Perfect with penne.

Cooking oil	2 tsp.	10 mL
Lean ground beef	1 lb.	454 g
Chopped onion	2 1/2 cups	625 mL
Chopped zucchini (with peel)	2 cups	500 mL
Quartered fresh white mushrooms	2 cups	500 mL
Chopped green pepper	1 3/4 cups	425 mL
Chopped yellow pepper	1 1/2 cups	375 mL
Can of tomato sauce	14 oz.	398 mL
Dried oregano	2 tsp.	10 mL
Salt	1/4 tsp.	1 mL
Pepper	1/8 tsp.	0.5 mL
Can of evaporated milk	13 1/2 oz.	385 mL
Grated Parmesan cheese	1/2 cup	125 mL
Chopped fresh basil	2 tbsp.	30 mL

Heat cooking oil in large deep frying pan or Dutch oven on medium. Add ground beef and onion. Scramble-fry for about 10 minutes until beef is no longer pink. Drain.

Add next 4 ingredients. Cook for about 10 minutes, stirring occasionally, until vegetables are tender-crisp.

Add next 4 ingredients. Stir. Bring to a boil on medium-high. Reduce heat to medium. Boil gently for about 10 minutes, stirring occasionally, until thickened.

Add evaporated milk. Heat and stir for 3 to 4 minutes until hot but not boiling. Remove to large serving bowl.

Sprinkle with Parmesan cheese and basil. Serves 6.

1 serving: 348 Calories; 16.6 g Total Fat (6.2 g Mono, 1.2 g Poly, 7.7 g Sat); 65 mg Cholesterol; 27 g Carbohydrate; 4 g Fibre; 25 g Protein; 795 mg Sodium

Caesar Meat Sauce

Spicy and hot! All the flavour of a well-known cocktail in a very thick, zesty meat sauce. Add your favourite pasta and toss.

Cooking oil	2 tsp.	10 mL
Lean ground beef	1 lb.	454 g
Chopped onion	1 cup	250 mL
Can of tomato sauce	14 oz.	398 mL
Lemon juice	1 tbsp.	15 mL
Granulated sugar	1 tbsp.	15 mL
Worcestershire sauce	1 tbsp.	15 mL
Hot pepper sauce	2 tsp.	10 mL
Celery salt	1/2 tsp.	2 mL
Pepper	1/2 tsp.	2 mL
Vodka (optional)	2 tbsp.	30 mL

Heat cooking oil in large frying pan on medium. Add ground beef and onion. Scramble-fry for about 10 minutes until beef is no longer pink. Drain.

Add next 7 ingredients. Stir. Bring to a boil. Reduce heat to medium-low. Simmer, uncovered, for 5 minutes, stirring occasionally.

Add vodka. Stir. Serves 4.

1 serving: 256 Calories; 12 g Total Fat (5.5 g Mono, 1.1 g Poly, 3.9 g Sat); 59 mg Cholesterol; 15 g Carbohydrate; 2 g Fibre; 23 g Protein; 926 mg Sodium

1. Chuckwagon Chipotle Chili, page 74
2. Cinnamon Chili, page 73
3. Five-Spice Hot Pot, page 141

Props courtesy of:
Cherison Enterprises Inc.

Cinnamon Chili

A taste adventure worth trying!

Cooking oil	2 tsp.	10 mL
Lean ground beef	1 lb.	454 g
Chopped onion	1 cup	250 mL
Garlic clove, minced (or 1/4 tsp., 1 mL, powder)	1	1
Chili powder	1 tbsp.	15 mL
Cocoa, sifted if lumpy	2 tsp.	10 mL
Ground cinnamon	1 tsp.	5 mL
Salt	1/2 tsp.	2 mL
Ground allspice	1/4 tsp.	1 mL
Bay leaf	1	1
Can of romano beans, rinsed and drained	19 oz.	540 mL
Can of diced tomatoes (with juice)	14 oz.	398 mL
Can of tomato sauce	7 1/2 oz.	213 mL
Water	1/2 cup	125 mL
Balsamic vinegar	1 tbsp.	15 mL

Heat cooking oil in large frying pan on medium. Add ground beef, onion and garlic. Scramble-fry for about 10 minutes until beef is no longer pink. Drain. Add next 6 ingredients. Heat and stir for about 1 minute until fragrant.

Add remaining 5 ingredients. Stir. Bring to a boil. Reduce heat to medium-low. Simmer, uncovered, for about 20 minutes, stirring occasionally, until slightly thickened. Discard bay leaf. Serves 6.

1 serving: 232 Calories; 8.8 g Total Fat (3.8 g Mono, 0.9 g Poly, 2.8 g Sat); 38 mg Cholesterol; 20 g Carbohydrate; 5 g Fibre; 19 g Protein; 686 mg Sodium

Pictured on page 71.

1. Meatballs In Curry Sauce, page 81
2. Tandoori Chili, page 68
3. Ground Beef Curry, page 140

Props courtesy of: Pier 1 Imports
　　　　　　　　The Dazzling Gourmet

Chuckwagon Chipotle Chili

Smoky flavour in warming chili. Potatoes are a hearty addition.
Great for a tailgate party or for a potluck picnic.

Cooking oil	2 tsp.	10 mL
Lean ground beef	1 lb.	454 g
Chopped onion	1 cup	250 mL
Chopped green pepper	1/2 cup	125 mL
Chipotle chili pepper in adobo sauce, chopped (see Tip, below)	1	1
Chili powder	2 tsp.	10 mL
Ground cumin	1/2 tsp.	2 mL
Salt	1/2 tsp.	2 mL
Bay leaf	1	1
Water	3 cups	750 mL
Can of black beans, rinsed and drained	19 oz.	540 mL
Can of diced tomatoes (with juice)	14 oz.	398 mL
Diced peeled potato	1 1/2 cups	375 mL
Frozen kernel corn	1 cup	250 mL
Can of tomato sauce	7 1/2 oz.	213 mL

Heat cooking oil in large deep frying pan or Dutch oven on medium. Add ground beef, onion and green pepper. Scramble-fry for about 10 minutes until beef is no longer pink. Drain.

Add next 5 ingredients. Heat and stir for about 1 minute until fragrant.

Add remaining 6 ingredients. Stir. Bring to a boil on medium-high. Reduce heat to medium. Boil gently, uncovered, for about 30 minutes, stirring occasionally, until potato is tender and sauce is thickened. Discard bay leaf. Serves 6.

1 serving: 290 Calories; 9 g Total Fat (3.9 g Mono, 1.1 g Poly, 2.8 g Sat); 38 mg Cholesterol; 34 g Carbohydrate; 5 g Fibre; 21 g Protein; 687 mg Sodium

Pictured on page 71.

 tip *Chipotle chili peppers are smoked jalapeño peppers. Be sure to wash your hands after handling. To store any leftover chipotle chili peppers, divide into recipe-friendly portions and freeze, with sauce, in airtight containers for up to one year.*

Chili Gumbo

Chili with a creole twist. If you like, add a few drops
of hot pepper sauce for extra heat. Serve with rice.

Bacon slices, diced	4	4
Lean ground beef	1 lb.	454 g
Chopped celery	1 cup	250 mL
Chopped onion	1/2 cup	125 mL
Can of diced tomatoes (with juice)	28 oz.	796 mL
Can of black-eyed peas, rinsed and drained	19 oz.	540 mL
Diced peeled yam (or sweet potato)	2 cups	500 mL
Can of crushed tomatoes	14 oz.	398 mL
Sliced fresh (or frozen, thawed) okra	1 1/2 cups	375 mL
Chopped green pepper	1 cup	250 mL
Prepared beef broth	1 cup	250 mL
Chili powder	1 tbsp.	15 mL
Dried oregano	1 tsp.	5 mL
Dried thyme	1 tsp.	5 mL
Garlic clove, minced (or 1/4 tsp., 1 mL, powder)	1	1
Dried basil	1/2 tsp.	2 mL
Salt	1/2 tsp.	2 mL
Cayenne pepper	1/8 tsp.	0.5 mL
Nutmeg, just a pinch		

Cook bacon in large deep frying pan or Dutch oven on medium until almost crisp.

Add ground beef, celery and onion. Scramble-fry for about 10 minutes until beef is no longer pink. Drain.

Add remaining 15 ingredients. Stir. Bring to a boil on medium-high. Reduce heat to medium-low. Simmer, covered, for about 30 minutes, stirring occasionally, until yam is tender and sauce is slightly thickened. Serves 6.

1 serving: 326 Calories; 9.8 g Total Fat (4 g Mono, 0.9 g Poly, 3.5 g Sat); 41 mg Cholesterol; 39 g Carbohydrate; 7 g Fibre; 22 g Protein; 908 mg Sodium

Pictured on front cover.

Chili And Dumplings

Traditional chunky chili crowned with fluffy dumplings.
A satisfying dish for lunch or dinner!

Cooking oil	2 tsp.	10 mL
Lean ground beef	1 lb.	454 g
Chopped onion	1 cup	250 mL
Garlic clove, minced (or 1/4 tsp., 1 mL, powder)	1	1
Chili powder	1 tbsp.	15 mL
Basil pesto	2 tsp.	10 mL
Ground cumin	1 tsp.	5 mL
Granulated sugar	1 tsp.	5 mL
Dried crushed chilies	1/2 tsp.	2 mL
Salt	1/2 tsp.	2 mL
Can of diced tomatoes (with juice)	14 oz.	398 mL
Can of red kidney beans, rinsed and drained	14 oz.	398 mL
Prepared beef broth	1 1/2 cups	375 mL
Can of tomato sauce	7 1/2 oz.	213 mL
CORNMEAL DUMPLINGS		
All-purpose flour	1/2 cup	125 mL
Yellow cornmeal	1/3 cup	75 mL
Grated Parmesan cheese	3 tbsp.	50 mL
Baking powder	1 tsp.	5 mL
Paprika	1/4 tsp.	1 mL
Large egg	1	1
Milk	2 tbsp.	30 mL
Cooking oil	2 tbsp.	30 mL
Basil pesto	1 tsp.	5 mL

Heat cooking oil in large deep frying pan or Dutch oven on medium. Add ground beef, onion and garlic. Scramble-fry for about 10 minutes until beef is no longer pink. Drain.

Add next 6 ingredients. Heat and stir for about 1 minute until fragrant.

Add next 4 ingredients. Stir. Bring to a boil. Reduce heat to medium-low. Simmer, uncovered, for 10 minutes, stirring occasionally.

(continued on next page)

Chilies & Sauces

Cornmeal Dumplings: Combine first 5 ingredients in medium bowl. Make a well in centre.

Beat remaining 4 ingredients with fork in small bowl until combined. Add to well. Stir until just moistened. Spoon mounds of batter, using about 2 tbsp. (30 mL) for each, in single layer on top of chili. Simmer, covered, for 15 to 20 minutes until wooden pick inserted in centre of dumpling comes out clean. Serves 6.

1 serving: 384 Calories; 16.2 g Total Fat (7.6 g Mono, 2.7 g Poly, 4.1 g Sat); 76 mg Cholesterol; 36 g Carbohydrate; 3 g Fibre; 24 g Protein; 1171 mg Sodium

Bolognese Sauce

This slow-cooker recipe can be adapted to a stovetop method.
Cook in a Dutch oven and simmer, covered, for about
an hour before adding the evaporated milk.

Olive (or cooking) oil	2 tsp.	10 mL
Chopped pancetta (or regular) bacon	4 oz.	113 g
Lean ground beef	2 lbs.	900 g
Finely chopped celery	2 cups	500 mL
Finely chopped carrot	2 cups	500 mL
Finely chopped onion	1 1/2 cups	375 mL
Prepared beef broth	2 cups	500 mL
Dry white (or alcohol-free) wine	1 cup	250 mL
Cans of tomato sauce (14 oz., 398 mL, each)	2	2
Can of evaporated milk	5 1/2 oz.	160 mL

Heat olive oil in large frying pan on medium. Add bacon. Cook for about 4 minutes, stirring occasionally, until almost crisp. Increase heat to medium-high.

Add next 4 ingredients. Scramble-fry for about 10 minutes until ground beef is no longer pink. Drain. Transfer to 4 to 5 quart (4 to 5 L) slow cooker.

Add next 3 ingredients. Stir. Cover. Cook on Low for 6 to 8 hours or on High for 3 to 4 hours. Skim any fat from surface of sauce.

Add evaporated milk. Stir. Cover. Cook on High for another 10 minutes until heated through. Serves 8.

1 serving: 318 Calories; 14.5 g Total Fat (6.5 g Mono, 0.9 g Poly, 5.6 g Sat); 68 mg Cholesterol; 17 g Carbohydrate; 3 g Fibre; 26 g Protein; 998 mg Sodium

Paprika Mushroom Sauce

*A mild, stroganoff-style sauce with the added tang of
artichokes. Delicious served over rice or egg noodles.*

Cooking oil	2 tsp.	10 mL
Lean ground beef	1 lb.	454 g
Cooking oil	1 tsp.	5 mL
Chopped fresh white mushrooms	3 cups	750 mL
Chopped onion	1 cup	250 mL
Paprika	4 tsp.	20 mL
Dry mustard	1 tsp.	5 mL
Pepper	1/4 tsp.	1 mL
All-purpose flour	1 tbsp.	15 mL
Prepared beef broth	2 cups	500 mL
Can of artichoke hearts, drained and quartered	14 oz.	398 mL
Can of diced tomatoes (with juice)	14 oz.	398 mL
Sour cream	1/2 cup	125 mL

Heat first amount of cooking oil in large frying pan or Dutch oven on medium. Add ground beef. Scramble-fry for about 10 minutes until no longer pink. Drain. Transfer to medium bowl. Cover to keep warm.

Heat second amount of cooking oil in same pan. Add next 5 ingredients. Cook for 5 to 10 minutes, stirring often, until onion is softened and liquid is evaporated.

Add flour. Heat and stir for 1 minute. Slowly add broth, stirring constantly. Heat and stir for about 5 minutes until boiling and thickened.

Add beef, artichoke hearts and tomatoes. Stir. Bring to a boil. Heat and stir for about 2 minutes until heated through.

Add sour cream. Heat and stir until hot but not boiling. Serves 4.

*1 serving: 364 Calories; 20 g Total Fat (8.6 g Mono, 2.4 g Poly, 7.1 g Sat); 69 mg Cholesterol;
21 g Carbohydrate; 5 g Fibre; 28 g Protein; 829 mg Sodium*

Tasty Meatballs

Keep these handy in the freezer to add to your favourite sauce or gravy for a meal that's ready in minutes. We've included them in Mushroom Sauce, page 80, Curry Sauce, page 81, and Pineapple Sauce, page 82.

White (or brown) bread slices, processed into crumbs	2	2
Finely chopped green onion	1/3 cup	75 mL
Milk	2 tbsp.	30 mL
Finely chopped fresh parsley (or 3/4 tsp., 4 mL, flakes)	1 tbsp.	15 mL
Garlic cloves, minced (or 1/2 tsp., 2 mL, powder)	2	2
Seasoned salt	1 tsp.	5 mL
Hot pepper sauce	1/2 tsp.	2 mL
Pepper	1/8 tsp.	0.5 mL
Lean ground beef	1 lb.	454 g

Combine all 8 ingredients in large bowl.

Add ground beef. Mix well. Roll into 1 1/2 inch (3.8 cm) balls. Arrange on greased baking sheet with sides. Bake in 400°F (205°C) oven for about 15 minutes until fully cooked, and internal temperature of beef reaches 160°F (71°C). Makes about 18 meatballs.

1 meatball: 48 Calories; 2.2 g Total Fat (1 g Mono, 0.1 g Poly, 0.9 g Sat); 13 mg Cholesterol; 2 g Carbohydrate; trace Fibre; 5 g Protein; 95 mg Sodium

Paré Pointer

I never repeat gossip, so listen carefully the first time.

Meatballs In Mushroom Sauce

*This silky, wine-infused mushroom sauce makes meatballs
a great go-together with mashed potatoes.*

Package of dried porcini mushrooms	3/4 oz.	22 g
Boiling water		
Hard margarine (or butter)	1 tbsp.	15 mL
Finely chopped onion	1/4 cup	60 mL
Dry white (or alcohol-free) wine	1/2 cup	125 mL
Parsley flakes	1/2 tsp.	2 mL
Dill weed	1/4 tsp.	1 mL
Pepper	1/4 tsp.	1 mL
All-purpose flour	1 1/2 tbsp.	25 mL
Block of cream cheese, cut up	4 oz.	125 g
Prepared beef broth	1 cup	250 mL
Milk	1 cup	250 mL

Tasty Meatballs (cooked), page 79

Put mushrooms into small bowl. Cover with boiling water. Let stand for about 20 minutes until softened. Drain. Rinse with cold water. Drain well. Finely chop. Set aside.

Melt margarine in large saucepan on medium. Add onion. Cook for 5 to 10 minutes, stirring often, until softened.

Add mushrooms and next 4 ingredients. Stir. Bring to a boil. Reduce heat to low. Simmer, uncovered, for about 3 minutes, stirring often, until liquid is evaporated.

Add flour. Heat and stir for 1 minute.

Add cream cheese. Heat and stir until melted. Slowly add broth, stirring constantly. Add milk. Heat and stir for about 4 minutes until boiling and thickened. Remove from heat.

Put Tasty Meatballs into ungreased 2 quart (2 L) casserole. Pour mushroom mixture over top. Stir until coated. Bake, uncovered, in 350°F (175°C) oven for about 40 minutes until meatballs are heated through. Serves 6.

1 serving: 434 Calories; 24.7 g Total Fat (9.6 g Mono, 1.2 g Poly, 11.8 g Sat); 96 mg Cholesterol; 20 g Carbohydrate; 1 g Fibre; 28 g Protein; 797 mg Sodium

Meatballs In Curry Sauce

*This meatball and tomato-based curry combination
is excellent served over rice or noodles.*

Cooking oil	3 tbsp.	50 mL
Finely chopped onion	1 1/2 cups	375 mL
Garlic cloves, minced	3	3
Finely grated, peeled gingerroot	2 tsp.	10 mL
Paprika	1 tsp.	5 mL
Turmeric	1 tsp.	5 mL
Ground coriander	1 tsp.	5 mL
Ground cumin	1 tsp.	5 mL
Salt	1/2 tsp.	2 mL
Dried crushed chilies	1/4 tsp.	1 mL
Ground cinnamon	1/8 tsp.	0.5 mL
Ground cloves, just a pinch		
Prepared beef broth	1 1/2 cups	375 mL
Can of tomato sauce	7 1/2 oz.	213 mL
Tasty Meatballs (cooked), page 79		
Plain yogurt	1/2 cup	125 mL

Heat cooking oil in large saucepan on medium. Add onion. Cook for 15 to 20 minutes, stirring often, until caramelized.

Add next 10 ingredients. Heat and stir for about 2 minutes until fragrant.

Add broth and tomato sauce. Stir. Bring to a boil.

Add Tasty Meatballs. Stir. Return to a boil. Reduce heat to medium-low. Simmer, uncovered, for about 45 minutes, stirring occasionally, until sauce is thickened.

Slowly add yogurt, stirring constantly. Heat and stir for about 1 minute until hot but not boiling. Serves 4.

1 serving: 257 Calories; 14.4 g Total Fat (7.2 g Mono, 2.5 g Poly, 3.4 g Sat); 41 mg Cholesterol; 15 g Carbohydrate; 2 g Fibre; 18 g Protein; 932 mg Sodium

Pictured on page 72.

Meatballs In Pineapple Sauce

This pineapple sauce, infused with chili and lime, adds an exotic flair to meatballs. A dominant ginger flavour makes this dish particularly delicious!

Cooking oil	1 tbsp.	15 mL
Finely chopped onion	1/3 cup	75 mL
Finely grated, peeled gingerroot	2 tsp.	10 mL
Can of crushed pineapple, drained and juice reserved	14 oz.	398 mL
Sweet chili sauce	1/2 cup	125 mL
Lime juice	3 tbsp.	50 mL
Minced crystallized ginger	1 tbsp.	15 mL
Soy sauce	2 tsp.	10 mL
Salt	1/4 tsp.	1 mL
Reserved pineapple juice	2/3 cup	150 mL
Cornstarch	2 tsp.	10 mL
Grated lime zest	1/4 tsp.	1 mL

Tasty Meatballs (cooked), page 79

Heat cooking oil in medium saucepan on medium. Add onion. Cook for about 2 minutes, stirring often, until starting to soften. Add ginger. Heat and stir for another 2 to 3 minutes until onion is softened.

Add next 6 ingredients. Stir. Bring to a boil.

Stir reserved pineapple juice and cornstarch in small bowl until smooth. Slowly add to crushed pineapple mixture, stirring constantly. Heat and stir for 2 to 3 minutes until boiling and slightly thickened.

Add lime zest. Stir. Remove from heat.

Put Tasty Meatballs into ungreased 2 quart (2 L) casserole. Pour pineapple mixture over top. Stir until coated. Bake, covered, in 325°F (160°C) oven for about 30 minutes until meatballs are heated through. Serves 6.

1 serving: 368 Calories; 13.7 g Total Fat (6.4 g Mono, 1.5 g Poly, 4.2 g Sat); 59 mg Cholesterol; 39 g Carbohydrate; 4 g Fibre; 24 g Protein; 1237 mg Sodium

Sesame Meatballs

These sesame-coated meatballs are tender on the inside and crunchy on the outside. Pickled ginger adds a tasty touch to the sauce.

Large egg	1	1
Soda cracker crumbs	1/3 cup	75 mL
Sliced green onion	1/4 cup	60 mL
Red curry paste	2 tsp.	10 mL
Salt	1/4 tsp.	1 mL
Pepper	1/4 tsp.	1 mL
Lean ground beef	1 lb.	454 g
Sesame seeds	2/3 cup	150 mL
SWEET AND SOUR SAUCE		
Pineapple juice	1/3 cup	75 mL
Soy sauce	1/4 cup	60 mL
Ketchup	1/4 cup	60 mL
Brown sugar, packed	1/4 cup	60 mL
Balsamic vinegar	2 tbsp.	30 mL
Chopped pickled ginger slices, drained	2 tbsp.	30 mL
Cornstarch	2 tsp.	10 mL

Combine first 6 ingredients in large bowl.

Add ground beef. Mix well. Roll into 1 inch (2.5 cm) balls.

Roll each meatball in sesame seeds in small shallow dish until coated. Arrange on greased baking sheet with sides. Bake in 350°F (175°C) oven for about 20 minutes until fully cooked, and internal temperature of beef reaches 160°F (71°C). Remove to large serving bowl. Cover to keep warm.

Sweet And Sour Sauce: Combine all 7 ingredients in small saucepan. Heat and stir on medium for 6 to 8 minutes until boiling and thickened. Makes about 1 cup (250 mL) sauce. Drizzle over meatballs, or serve on the side. Serves 4.

1 serving: 328 Calories; 16.7 g Total Fat (6.8 g Mono, 4.3 g Poly, 4 g Sat); 75 mg Cholesterol; 27 g Carbohydrate; 4 g Fibre; 20 g Protein; 1068 mg Sodium

Pictured on page 89.

Spicy Lava Meatballs

A spicy cheese surprise oozes like lava from these meatballs—an explosion of flavour kids of all ages will enjoy. Serve these as soon as they're cooked for best effect.

Grated Monterey Jack With Jalapeño cheese	1 cup	250 mL
Block of cream cheese, softened	4 oz.	125 g
Crushed buttery crackers	1/4 cup	60 mL
Cajun seasoning	2 tsp.	10 mL
Large egg	1	1
Crushed buttery crackers	1/2 cup	125 mL
Finely chopped green onion	2 tbsp.	30 mL
Worcestershire sauce	1 tbsp.	15 mL
Prepared horseradish	2 tsp.	10 mL
Lean ground beef	1 1/2 lbs.	680 g

Combine first 4 ingredients in small bowl. Roll cheese mixture into 18 inch (45 cm) log. Cut into 1/2 inch (12 mm) slices, for a total of 36 slices. Roll each slice into ball. Arrange on ungreased baking sheet. Freeze for about 1 hour until firm.

Combine next 5 ingredients in large bowl.

Add ground beef. Mix well. Divide into 36 equal portions. Roll into balls. Dent each ball with thumb. Place 1 cheese ball into each dent. Re-roll each ball to completely cover cheese ball with beef mixture. Arrange on greased baking sheet with sides. Broil on top rack in oven for about 15 minutes until fully cooked, and internal temperature of beef reaches 160°F (71°C). Cheese should be oozing from meatballs. Serve immediately. Makes 36 meatballs.

1 meatball: 69 Calories; 4.6 g Total Fat (1.7 g Mono, 0.4 g Poly, 2.2 g Sat); 22 mg Cholesterol; 2 g Carbohydrate; trace Fibre; 5 g Protein; 68 mg Sodium

Vietnamese Noodle Balls

Serve these unique meatballs as an appetizer, or add them to a stir-fry of vegetables and hoisin sauce.

Rice vermicelli	2 oz.	57 g
Hot water		
Large egg, fork-beaten	1	1
Sliced green onion	3 tbsp.	50 mL
Soy sauce	2 tbsp.	30 mL
Fish sauce	2 tbsp.	30 mL
Cornstarch	2 tbsp.	30 mL
Medium sherry	1 tbsp.	15 mL
Garlic clove, minced (or 1/4 tsp., 1 mL, powder)	1	1
Granulated sugar	1 tsp.	5 mL
Sesame oil, for flavour	1 tsp.	5 mL
Pepper	1/2 tsp.	2 mL
Lean ground beef	1 lb.	454 g

Put vermicelli into large bowl. Cover with hot water. Let stand for about 5 minutes until softened. Drain. Coarsely chop. Return to same bowl.

Add next 10 ingredients. Stir.

Add ground beef. Mix well. Roll into 1 inch (2.5 cm) balls. Arrange on greased baking sheet with sides. Bake in 350°F (175°C) oven for 20 to 25 minutes until fully cooked, and internal temperature of beef reaches 160°F (71°C). Makes about 36 meatballs.

1 meatball: 33 Calories; 1.3 g Total Fat (0.6 g Mono, 0.1 g Poly, 0.5 g Sat); 12 mg Cholesterol; 2 g Carbohydrate; 0 g Fibre; 3 g Protein; 123 mg Sodium

Apricot Meatballs

Chewy apricot is hidden inside meatballs
coated with a sweet, smoky sauce. So good!

Dried apricots, halved	18	18
Water		
Large egg	1	1
Finely chopped onion	1/4 cup	60 mL
Cornflake crumbs	1/4 cup	60 mL
Worcestershire sauce	1 tsp.	5 mL
Dried rosemary, crushed	1/2 tsp.	2 mL
Lean ground beef	1 lb.	454 g
APRICOT SAUCE		
Apricot jam	1/2 cup	125 mL
Hickory barbecue sauce	1/4 cup	60 mL
Apple cider vinegar	1 tbsp.	15 mL

Put apricot halves into medium bowl. Cover with water. Let stand for 10 to 15 minutes until softened. Drain. Squeeze out excess water. Blot dry with paper towels. Set aside.

Combine next 5 ingredients in medium bowl.

Add ground beef. Mix well. Divide into 36 equal portions. Roll into balls. Dent each ball with thumb. Place 1 apricot half into each dent. Re-roll each ball to completely cover apricot with beef mixture. Arrange on greased baking sheet with sides. Bake in 400°F (205°C) oven for about 15 minutes until fully cooked, and internal temperature of beef reaches 160°F (71°C). Transfer to greased 2 quart (2 L) casserole.

Apricot Sauce: Combine jam, barbecue sauce and vinegar in small saucepan. Heat and stir on medium for about 3 minutes until heated through. Makes about 1 cup (250 mL) sauce. Pour over meatballs. Stir until coated. Bake, covered, in 350°F (175°C) oven for about 20 minutes until sauce is boiling. Serves 4.

1 serving: 373 Calories; 11.2 g Total Fat (4.8 g Mono, 0.6 g Poly, 4.1 g Sat); 112 mg Cholesterol; 46 g Carbohydrate; 3 g Fibre; 24 g Protein; 290 mg Sodium

Pictured on page 89.

Nacho Meatballs

These Tex-Mex meatballs smothered with spicy cheese sauce are sure to become a favourite. Serve with rice, or tuck the meatballs and sauce inside taco shells or pita breads.

Large egg	1	1
Crushed nacho chips	1/2 cup	125 mL
Medium salsa	1/4 cup	60 mL
Envelope of taco seasoning mix	1 1/4 oz.	35 g
Lean ground beef	1 lb.	454 g
NACHO CHEESE SAUCE		
Hard margarine (or butter)	2 tbsp.	30 mL
All-purpose flour	2 tbsp.	30 mL
Dry mustard	1/2 tsp.	2 mL
Cayenne pepper	1/8 tsp.	0.5 mL
Milk	1 cup	250 mL
Grated sharp Cheddar cheese	1 cup	250 mL

Combine first 4 ingredients in medium bowl.

Add ground beef. Mix well. Roll into 1 inch (2.5 cm) balls. Arrange on greased baking sheet with sides. Bake in 350°F (175°C) oven for about 15 minutes until fully cooked, and internal temperature of beef reaches 160°F (71°C). Remove to large serving bowl. Cover to keep warm.

Nacho Cheese Sauce: Melt margarine in small saucepan on medium. Add flour, mustard and cayenne pepper. Heat and stir for 1 minute.

Slowly add milk, stirring constantly. Heat and stir for about 5 minutes until boiling and thickened. Remove from heat.

Add cheese. Stir until melted. Makes about 1 1/3 cups (325 mL) sauce. Pour over meatballs, or serve on the side. Serves 6.

1 serving: 310 Calories; 19.6 g Total Fat (8.3 g Mono, 1.1 g Poly, 8.2 g Sat); 98 mg Cholesterol; 11 g Carbohydrate; 1 g Fibre; 22 g Protein; 951 mg Sodium

Salsa Porcupines

Forget the chicken dance, these porcupines like to salsa! Old-fashioned meatballs are smothered in a tangy sauce and topped with cheese.

Long grain white rice	1/2 cup	125 mL
Milk	1/2 cup	125 mL
Finely chopped onion	1/4 cup	60 mL
Salt	1 tsp.	5 mL
Pepper	1/4 tsp.	1 mL
Lean ground beef	1 lb.	454 g
Mild salsa	2 cups	500 mL
Water	1/2 cup	125 mL
Grated Monterey Jack cheese	1/2 cup	125 mL

Combine first 5 ingredients in large bowl.

Add ground beef. Mix well. Roll into 1 1/2 inch (3.8 cm) balls. Arrange in greased 9 x 9 inch (22 x 22 cm) pan.

Combine salsa and water in medium bowl. Pour over meatballs. Cover with foil. Bake in 400°F (205°C) oven for about 1 1/4 hours until fully cooked, and internal temperature of beef reaches 160°F (71°C).

Sprinkle with cheese. Serves 4.

1 serving: 438 Calories; 22.5 g Total Fat (8.9 g Mono, 1.1 g Poly, 10 g Sat); 78 mg Cholesterol; 29 g Carbohydrate; 3 g Fibre; 29 g Protein; 1120 mg Sodium

1. Saffron Meatball Casserole, page 39
2. Apricot Meatballs, page 86
3. Sweet and Sour Sauce, page 83
4. Sesame Meatballs, page 83
5. Grilled Meatball Skewers, page 92

Props courtesy of:
Anchor Hocking Canada

Cherison Enterprisesu Inc.

Danesco Inc.

Ginger Meatballs

When you're looking for a taste of the Orient, these meatballs are the ones to try. Add them to stir-fry veggies, or serve them with rice.

Large egg	1	1
Crisp rice cereal	1 cup	250 mL
Ketchup	1/4 cup	60 mL
Jar of pickled ginger slices, drained and finely chopped	1 3/4 oz.	50 g
Finely chopped onion	2 tbsp.	30 mL
Prepared horseradish	1 tbsp.	15 mL
Soy sauce	1 tbsp.	15 mL
Balsamic vinegar	1 tbsp.	15 mL
Lean ground beef	1 lb.	454 g

Combine first 8 ingredients in large bowl.

Add ground beef. Mix well. Roll into 1 1/2 inch (3.8 cm) balls. Arrange on greased baking sheet with sides. Bake in 400°F (205°C) oven for about 20 minutes until fully cooked, and internal temperature of beef reaches 160°F (71°C). Makes about 20 meatballs.

1 meatball: 51 Calories; 2.2 g Total Fat (0.9 g Mono, 0.1 g Poly, 0.8 g Sat); 22 mg Cholesterol; 3 g Carbohydrate; trace Fibre; 5 g Protein; 118 mg Sodium

1. Beef And Vegetable Roundup, page 96
2. Gourmet Mini-Meatloaves, page 100
3. Layered Cajun Loaf, page 99

Props courtesy of: Cherison Enterprises Inc.
Danesco Inc.

Grilled Meatball Skewers

For an attractive presentation, arrange these tri-coloured skewers
on a bed of coconut rice. Serve with peanut sauce for dipping.

Large egg	1	1
Graham cracker crumbs	1/3 cup	75 mL
Smooth peanut butter	2 tbsp.	30 mL
Soy sauce	1 tbsp.	15 mL
Garlic clove, minced (or 1/4 tsp., 1 mL, powder)	1	1
Curry powder	1 tsp.	5 mL
Ground ginger	1/2 tsp.	2 mL
Coconut flavouring	1/2 tsp.	2 mL
Lean ground beef	1 lb.	454 g
Can of pineapple chunks, drained	14 oz.	398 mL
Large red pepper, cut into 24 equal pieces	1	1
Bamboo skewers (8 inches, 20 cm, each), soaked in water for 10 minutes	8	8

Combine first 8 ingredients in medium bowl.

Add ground beef. Mix well. Divide into 24 equal portions. Roll into balls.

Thread pineapple, red pepper and meatballs alternately onto skewers, beginning and ending with pineapple on each (see photo, page 89). Preheat gas barbecue to medium. (For other cooking methods, see page 8.) Cook skewers on greased grill for 12 to 15 minutes, turning occasionally, until fully cooked and internal temperature of beef reaches 160°F (71°C). Makes 8 skewers.

1 skewer: 161 Calories; 8.1 g Total Fat (3.6 g Mono, 0.9 g Poly, 2.6 g Sat); 55 mg Cholesterol; 10 g Carbohydrate; 1 g Fibre; 13 g Protein; 210 mg Sodium

Pictured on page 89.

APPETIZER MEATBALL SKEWERS: Soak twenty-four 4 inch (10 cm) bamboo skewers in water for 10 minutes. Thread 1 meatball, 1 pineapple chunk and 1 red pepper piece onto each. Cook as directed.

Meatloaf Classic

*A favourite from Casseroles, this good
old-fashioned meatloaf will be a hit with
kids and adults alike. Great comfort food!*

Large egg	1	1
Quick-cooking rolled oats	3/4 cup	175 mL
Milk	3/4 cup	175 mL
Minced onion (or 1 tbsp., 15 mL, onion flakes)	1/4 cup	60 mL
Parsley flakes	1 tsp.	5 mL
Worcestershire sauce	1 tsp.	5 mL
Salt	1 1/2 tsp.	7 mL
Pepper	1/4 tsp.	1 mL
Lean ground beef	1 1/2 lbs.	680 g
Grated medium Cheddar cheese	1 cup	250 mL
Ketchup	1/4 cup	60 mL

Combine first 8 ingredients in large bowl.

Add ground beef. Mix well. Press 1/2 of beef mixture into greased
9 × 5 × 3 inch (22 × 12.5 × 7.5 cm) loaf pan.

Sprinkle with cheese. Press remaining beef mixture on top of cheese.

Spread ketchup on top of beef mixture. Bake, uncovered, in 350°F (175°C)
oven for 1 1/4 to 1 1/2 hours until fully cooked, and internal temperature
of beef reaches 160°F (71°C). Let stand for 10 minutes. Cuts into 12 slices.
Serves 6.

*1 serving: 416 Calories; 25.8 g Total Fat (10 g Mono, 1.4 g Poly, 11.7 g Sat); 122 mg Cholesterol;
14 g Carbohydrate; 2 g Fibre; 30 g Protein; 955 mg Sodium*

Paré Pointer

*He offered his girlfriend anything she wanted,
so she took everything he had—including his best friend!*

Sweet Onion Loaf

Sweet caramelized onions are baked into this savoury
meatloaf. Topped nicely with a zippy mustard glaze.

Hard margarine (or butter)	2 tbsp.	30 mL
Olive (or cooking) oil	1 tbsp.	15 mL
Thinly sliced onion	2 cups	500 mL
Balsamic vinegar	1 tbsp.	15 mL
Large egg	1	1
Fine dry bread crumbs	1/2 cup	125 mL
Garlic clove, minced (or 1/4 tsp., 1 mL, powder)	1	1
Dried thyme	1/2 tsp.	2 mL
Seasoned salt	1/2 tsp.	2 mL
Pepper	1/4 tsp.	1 mL
Lean ground beef	2 lbs.	900 g
Dijon mustard	2 tbsp.	30 mL
Liquid honey	2 tbsp.	30 mL
Prepared mustard	1 tbsp.	15 mL

Heat margarine and olive oil in medium frying pan on medium. Add onion. Cook for 15 to 20 minutes, stirring often, until caramelized.

Add vinegar. Stir. Remove from heat.

Combine next 6 ingredients in large bowl.

Add caramelized onion and ground beef. Mix well. Press into greased 9 x 5 x 3 inch (22 x 12.5 x 7.5 cm) loaf pan. Bake, uncovered, in 350°F (175°C) oven for 30 minutes. Drain.

Combine last 3 ingredients in small cup. Spread on top of meatloaf. Bake for another 25 to 30 minutes until fully cooked, and internal temperature of beef reaches 160°F (71°C). Let stand for 10 minutes. Cuts into 8 slices.

1 slice: 362 Calories; 23.1 g Total Fat (11.1 g Mono, 1.5 g Poly, 8 g Sat); 91 mg Cholesterol; 14 g Carbohydrate; 1 g Fibre; 24 g Protein; 331 mg Sodium

Ground Beef Pot Roast

Easy to make and easy to serve. This homestyle meatloaf
"pot roast," seasoned with horseradish, is a complete meal.

Large eggs	2	2
Quick-cooking rolled oats	3/4 cup	175 mL
Water	1/3 cup	75 mL
Envelope of dry onion soup mix	1 1/2 oz.	42 g
Prepared horseradish	1 tbsp.	15 mL
Pepper	1/2 tsp.	2 mL
Extra-lean ground beef	1 1/2 lbs.	680 g
Baby carrots	3 cups	750 mL
Cubed peeled potato	3 cups	750 mL
Thinly sliced onion	1 1/2 cups	375 mL

Combine first 6 ingredients in large bowl.

Add ground beef. Mix well. Shape into 4 × 6 inch (10 × 15 cm) oval. Put into greased medium roasting pan.

Arrange remaining 3 ingredients around meatloaf in pan. Bake, covered, in 350°F (175°C) oven for 1 hour. Remove cover. Bake for another 20 to 30 minutes until fully cooked, and internal temperature of beef reaches 160°F (71°C). Serves 6.

1 serving: 471 Calories; 19.3 g Total Fat (8.2 g Mono, 1.3 g Poly, 7.1 g Sat); 148 mg Cholesterol; 39 g Carbohydrate; 5 g Fibre; 35 g Protein; 739 mg Sodium

Paré Pointer
You can tell when the sun gets tired—it sets for awhile.

Beef And Vegetable Roundup

This unique meatloaf is great for a casual dinner. A hint of
hickory and a layer of crunchy veggies are rolled up inside.

Large eggs	2	2
Fine dry bread crumbs	2/3 cup	150 mL
Ketchup	1/3 cup	75 mL
Seasoned salt	1 1/2 tsp.	7 mL
Pepper	1/2 tsp.	2 mL
Lean ground beef	2 lbs.	900 g
Thinly sliced onion	1 cup	250 mL
Grated carrot	1 cup	250 mL
Grated zucchini, squeezed dry	1 cup	250 mL
Fine dry bread crumbs	1/3 cup	75 mL
Hickory barbecue sauce	3 tbsp.	50 mL
Ketchup	2 tbsp.	30 mL
Parsley flakes	2 tsp.	10 mL
Hickory barbecue sauce	3 tbsp.	50 mL
Ketchup	2 tbsp.	30 mL

Combine first 5 ingredients in large bowl.

Add ground beef. Mix well. On large sheet of foil, pat out beef mixture to 10 × 15 inch (25 × 38 cm) rectangle.

Combine next 7 ingredients in large bowl. Spread on top of beef rectangle, leaving 1 inch (2.5 cm) edge on 1 long side. Roll up from uncovered long side, jelly-roll style, using foil as guide. Press seam against roll to seal. Place, seam-side down, on greased baking sheet with sides. Bake, uncovered, in 350°F (175°C) oven for 30 minutes.

Combine second amount of barbecue sauce and third amount of ketchup in small cup. Spread on top of meatloaf. Bake for another 25 to 30 minutes until fully cooked, and internal temperature of beef reaches 160°F (71°C). Let stand for 10 minutes. Cuts into 8 slices.

1 slice: 291 Calories; 11.7 g Total Fat (5 g Mono, 0.9 g Poly, 4.3 g Sat); 112 mg Cholesterol; 21 g Carbohydrate; 3 g Fibre; 25 g Protein; 722 mg Sodium

Pictured on page 90.

Ricotta Swiss Wedges

A meatloaf that looks like a cake! You can garnish each wedge with a potato rosette and top with a cherry tomato— kids will love a meal that looks like dessert.

Large eggs	2	2
Bacon slices, cooked crisp and crumbled	4	4
Fine dry bread crumbs	3/4 cup	175 mL
Tomato sauce	1/2 cup	125 mL
Medium salsa	1/2 cup	125 mL
Dried basil	1/2 tsp.	2 mL
Dried oregano	1/4 tsp.	1 mL
Dried thyme	1/4 tsp.	1 mL
Salt	1/4 tsp.	1 mL
Pepper	1/4 tsp.	1 mL
Lean ground beef	1 lb.	454 g
Lean ground pork	1/2 lb.	225 g
Ricotta cheese	2 cups	500 mL
Grated Swiss cheese	1 cup	250 mL
Chopped fresh parsley (or 3/4 tsp., 4 mL, flakes)	1 tbsp.	15 mL

Combine first 10 ingredients in large bowl.

Add ground beef and pork. Mix well. Press into greased 9 inch (22 cm) springform pan. Set pan on baking sheet with sides. Bake, uncovered, in 350°F (175°C) oven for about 30 minutes until firm.

Combine remaining 3 ingredients in small bowl. Spread on top of meatloaf. Bake for another 45 to 50 minutes until fully cooked, and internal temperature of meat reaches 160°F (71°C). Let stand for 10 minutes. Cuts into 8 wedges.

1 wedge: 399 Calories; 24.6 g Total Fat (8.7 g Mono, 1.5 g Poly, 12.4 g Sat); 150 mg Cholesterol; 13 g Carbohydrate; 1 g Fibre; 31 g Protein; 503 mg Sodium

Pictured on page 53 and on back cover.

Spinach-Stuffed Meatloaf

Looks as good as it tastes! Stuffed with bacon and spinach and glazed with apricot jam, this meatloaf has a delightfully sweet, smoky flavour.

Bacon slices, diced	4	4
Chopped onion	1/2 cup	125 mL
Garlic clove, minced (or 1/4 tsp., 1 mL, powder)	1	1
Box of frozen chopped spinach, thawed and squeezed dry	10 oz.	300 g
Chopped dried apricot	1/4 cup	60 mL
Pepper	1/2 tsp.	2 mL
Large egg	1	1
Crushed buttery crackers	1/2 cup	125 mL
Balsamic vinegar	2 tbsp.	30 mL
Seasoned salt	1/2 tsp.	2 mL
Lean ground beef	1 lb.	454 g
Apricot jam	1/4 cup	60 mL
Apple cider vinegar	1 1/2 tbsp.	25 mL

Cook bacon in medium frying pan on medium until crisp. Transfer with slotted spoon to paper towels to drain. Set aside.

Heat 1 tbsp. (15 mL) drippings in same pan on medium. Add onion and garlic. Heat and stir for about 3 minutes until onion starts to soften.

Add next 3 ingredients. Stir. Remove from heat. Set aside.

Combine next 4 ingredients in medium bowl. Add ground beef. Mix well. On large sheet of foil, pat out beef mixture to 8 x 11 inch (20 x 28 cm) rectangle. Spoon spinach mixture lengthwise along centre of rectangle. Sprinkle bacon over top. Fold both long sides over stuffing to enclose. Pinch edges to seal. Holding foil, carefully roll meatloaf onto greased wire rack set on greased baking sheet with sides. Seam side should be down. Discard foil. Bake, uncovered, in 350°F (175°C) oven for 30 minutes.

Combine jam and apple cider vinegar in small cup. Spread on top of meatloaf. Bake for another 10 to 15 minutes until fully cooked, and internal temperature of beef reaches 160°F (71°C). Let stand for 10 minutes. Cuts into 8 slices.

1 slice: 225 Calories; 12.3 g Total Fat (5.3 g Mono, 1.1 g Poly, 4.5 g Sat); 62 mg Cholesterol; 15 g Carbohydrate; 1 g Fibre; 14 g Protein; 238 mg Sodium

Pictured on front cover.

Layered Cajun Loaf

Spicy and delicious. Great with rice and steamed veggies.

Large egg	1	1
Grated Monterey Jack cheese	1 cup	250 mL
Soda cracker crumbs	1/2 cup	125 mL
Can of diced green chilies	4 oz.	113 g
Dried thyme	1/4 tsp.	1 mL
Ground coriander	1/4 tsp.	1 mL
Ground marjoram	1/4 tsp.	1 mL
Large egg	1	1
Finely chopped onion	1 cup	250 mL
Soda cracker crumbs	2/3 cup	150 mL
Tomato sauce	1/3 cup	75 mL
Garlic clove, minced (or 1/4 tsp., 1 mL, powder)	1	1
Salt	1/2 tsp.	2 mL
Pepper	1/2 tsp.	2 mL
Lean ground beef	1 1/4 lbs.	560 g
Tomato sauce	1/2 cup	125 mL
Cajun seasoning	1/2 tsp.	2 mL

Combine first 7 ingredients in medium bowl. Divide into 2 equal portions. Set aside.

Combine next 7 ingredients in large bowl.

Add ground beef. Mix well. Divide into 3 equal portions. Starting and ending with beef mixture, press portions of beef and cheese mixtures alternately into greased 9 x 5 x 3 inch (22 x 12.5 x 7.5 cm) loaf pan. Press down lightly. Bake, uncovered, in 350°F (175°C) oven for 30 minutes.

Stir second amount of tomato sauce and seasoning in small bowl. Spread on top of meatloaf. Bake for another 30 to 35 minutes until fully cooked, and internal temperature of beef reaches 160°F (71°C). Let stand for 10 minutes. Cuts into 6 slices.

1 slice: 399 Calories; 23.9 g Total Fat (9.6 g Mono, 1.4 g Poly, 10.3 g Sat); 142 mg Cholesterol; 18 g Carbohydrate; 2 g Fibre; 27 g Protein; 826 mg Sodium

Pictured on page 90.

Gourmet Mini-Meatloaves

Elegant individual meatloaves infused with rich, Italian flavours.
When company's coming, these are sure to impress!

Large egg	1	1
Balsamic vinegar	3 tbsp.	50 mL
Crushed seasoned croutons	1/2 cup	125 mL
Lean ground beef	1 1/2 lbs.	680 g
Block of cream cheese, softened	4 oz.	125 g
Finely chopped prosciutto (or deli) ham	1/2 cup	125 mL
Grated Parmesan cheese	1/3 cup	75 mL
Sun-dried tomato pesto	3 tbsp.	50 mL
Chopped fresh sage (or 3/4 tsp., 4 mL, dried)	1 tbsp.	15 mL
SUN-DRIED TOMATO SAUCE		
Diced Roma (plum) tomato	1 3/4 cups	425 mL
Prepared chicken broth	1 1/4 cups	300 mL
Chopped green onion	1/2 cup	125 mL
Sun-dried tomato pesto	1/4 cup	60 mL
Water	1 tbsp.	15 mL
Cornstarch	1 tbsp.	15 mL

Combine first 3 ingredients in large bowl.

Add ground beef. Mix well. Divide into 8 equal portions. Press into 8 greased 1/2 cup (125 mL) ramekins. Make a well in each, about 1 1/2 inches (3.8 cm) in diameter and 1 inch (2.5 cm) deep.

Combine next 5 ingredients in small bowl. Spoon about 2 tbsp. (30 mL) cheese mixture into each well. Place ramekins on baking sheet. Cover with greased foil. Bake in 350°F (175°C) oven for about 40 minutes until fully cooked, and internal temperature of beef reaches 160°F (71°C). Cool slightly. Lift meatloaves from ramekins to paper towels to drain. Cover to keep warm.

Sun-Dried Tomato Sauce: Combine first 4 ingredients in small saucepan. Bring to a boil on medium. Boil gently for about 5 minutes, stirring occasionally, until tomato is softened.

(continued on next page)

Stir water and cornstarch in small cup until smooth. Slowly add to tomato mixture, stirring constantly. Heat and stir for about 1 minute until boiling and thickened. Makes about 2 1/3 cups (575 mL) sauce. Put meatloaves on dinner plates. Spoon sauce over top. Serves 8.

1 serving: 342 Calories; 23.4 g Total Fat (9.4 g Mono, 1.3 g Poly, 10.4 g Sat); 101 mg Cholesterol; 9 g Carbohydrate; 1 g Fibre; 23 g Protein; 530 mg Sodium

Pictured on page 90.

Lazy Stuffed Meatloaf

A 1950s-style meatloaf, complete with ketchup glaze.
Add some mashed potatoes and you've got comfort food at its best.

Large egg	1	1
Tomato juice	1 cup	250 mL
Fine dry bread crumbs	1/2 cup	125 mL
Finely chopped onion	1/2 cup	125 mL
Prepared horseradish	1 tsp.	5 mL
Celery salt	1/2 tsp.	2 mL
Salt	1/2 tsp.	2 mL
Pepper	1/4 tsp.	1 mL
Box of chicken stove-top stuffing mix, prepared according to package directions	4 1/4 oz.	120 g
Lean ground beef	1 lb.	454 g
Ketchup	3 tbsp.	50 mL
Mustard	1 tbsp.	15 mL

Combine first 8 ingredients in large bowl.

Add prepared stuffing. Stir. Add ground beef. Mix well. Press into greased 2 quart (2 L) casserole.

Combine ketchup and mustard in small cup. Spread on top of beef mixture. Bake, uncovered, in 350°F (175°C) oven for about 1 hour until fully cooked, and internal temperature of beef reaches 160°F (71°C). Serves 6.

1 serving: 362 Calories; 19.1 g Total Fat (8.2 g Mono, 2.7 g Poly, 6.2 g Sat); 79 mg Cholesterol; 28 g Carbohydrate; 3 g Fibre; 19 g Protein; 1103 mg Sodium

Italian Sandwich

Tell your guests to bring their appetite! These attractive,
open-face sandwiches are loaded with Italian flavour.

BRUSCHETTA TOPPING

Diced tomato	3 cups	750 mL
Finely chopped green onion	1/3 cup	75 mL
Chopped fresh basil (or 3/4 tsp., 4 mL, dried)	1 tbsp.	15 mL
Garlic clove, minced (or 1/4 tsp., 1 mL, powder)	1	1
Dried oregano	1/2 tsp.	2 mL
Salt, just a pinch		
Pepper, just a pinch		
Large egg	1	1
Crushed Caesar croutons	1/2 cup	125 mL
Garlic clove, minced (or 1/4 tsp., 1 mL, powder)	1	1
Dried oregano	1/2 tsp.	2 mL
Salt	1/8 tsp.	0.5 mL
Pepper	1/8 tsp.	0.5 mL
Lean ground beef	1 lb.	454 g
Ciabatta rolls (see Note), split	2	2
Balsamic vinegar	2 tbsp.	30 mL
Olive oil	1 tbsp.	15 mL
Provolone (or process mozzarella) cheese slices	8	8

Bruschetta Topping: Combine first 7 ingredients in medium bowl. Makes about 3 1/2 cups (875 mL) topping.

Combine next 6 ingredients in large bowl. Add ground beef. Mix well. Divide into 4 equal portions. Shape into oval patties to fit ciabatta rolls. Place patties on greased baking sheet with sides. Broil on centre rack in oven for 5 to 7 minutes per side until fully cooked, and internal temperature of beef reaches 160°F (71°C).

Place rolls, cut-side up, on separate baking sheet. Brush with vinegar and olive oil. Top each half with 1 patty, Bruschetta Topping and 2 cheese slices. Broil on centre rack for 4 to 5 minutes until cheese is melted and golden. Serves 4.

(continued on next page)

1 serving: 619 Calories; 40.5 g Total Fat (15.9 g Mono, 2.1 g Poly, 18.8 g Sat); 160 mg Cholesterol; 21 g Carbohydrate; 2 g Fibre; 42 g Protein; 903 mg Sodium

Pictured on page 107.

Note: If ciabatta rolls are not available in your grocery store, use other crusty, dense rolls that will support the moist topping without becoming soggy.

Pesto Goat Cheese Wedges

A round loaf of savoury bread holds a large patty. Individual wedges are an attractive, tasty alternative to the traditional hamburger.

Fine dry bread crumbs	1/4 cup	60 mL
Grated Parmesan cheese	3 tbsp.	50 mL
Basil pesto	3 tbsp.	50 mL
Pepper	1/2 tsp.	2 mL
Lean ground beef	1 lb.	454 g
Goat (chèvre) cheese	3/4 cup	175 mL
Mayonnaise	1/4 cup	60 mL
Roasted red peppers, drained, blotted dry, finely chopped	3 tbsp.	50 mL
Herb focaccia bread (10 inch, 25 cm, diameter)	1	1
Shredded lettuce, lightly packed	1 cup	250 mL

Combine first 4 ingredients in medium bowl.

Add ground beef. Mix well. Roll into ball. Place on ungreased 12 inch (30 cm) pizza pan or on baking sheet with sides. Pat out to 10 inch (25 cm) diameter patty. Bake in 350°F (175°C) oven for about 15 minutes until fully cooked, and internal temperature of beef reaches 160°F (71°C). Transfer to large plate. Cover to keep warm.

Combine next 3 ingredients in small bowl.

Cut focaccia bread in half horizontally. Spread goat cheese mixture on both halves. Scatter lettuce over cheese mixture on bottom half. Carefully slide patty onto lettuce. Cover with top half of bread. Cuts into 6 wedges.

1 wedge: 537 Calories; 27.4 g Total Fat (12 g Mono, 4.8 g Poly, 8.7 g Sat); 63 mg Cholesterol; 44 g Carbohydrate; 2 g Fibre; 27 g Protein; 942 mg Sodium

Hummus Pita Pockets

Hummus gives the patties a velvety texture, while the cooling cucumber sauce completes the Mediterranean influence on these scrumptious pitas.

CUCUMBER DILL SAUCE

Plain yogurt	1/2 cup	125 mL
Finely chopped English cucumber (with peel)	1/2 cup	125 mL
Chopped fresh dill (or 3/4 tsp., 4 mL, dill weed)	1 tbsp.	15 mL
Lemon juice	2 tsp.	10 mL
Garlic clove, minced (or 1/4 tsp., 1 mL, powder)	1	1
Large egg	1	1
Hummus	1/3 cup	75 mL
Fine dry bread crumbs	1/4 cup	60 mL
Milk	2 tbsp.	30 mL
Dried oregano	1/2 tsp.	2 mL
Ground cumin	1/2 tsp.	2 mL
Lean ground beef	1 lb.	454 g
Pita breads (7 inch, 18 cm, diameter)	2	2
Shredded iceberg lettuce, lightly packed	1 cup	250 mL

Cucumber Dill Sauce: Combine first 5 ingredients in medium bowl. Chill. Makes about 7/8 cup (200 mL) sauce.

Combine next 6 ingredients in large bowl.

Add ground beef. Mix well. Divide into 4 equal portions. Shape into 1/2 inch (12 mm) thick oval patties. Preheat gas barbecue to medium. (For other cooking methods, see page 8.) Cook patties on greased grill for 6 to 8 minutes per side until fully cooked, and internal temperature of beef reaches 160°F (71°C). Transfer to large plate. Cover to keep warm.

Cut pita breads in half crosswise. Fill each half with 1/4 cup (60 mL) lettuce and 1 patty. Spoon sauce over patties. Makes 4 pita pockets.

1 pita pocket: 406 Calories; 16.3 g Total Fat (7.3 g Mono, 1.8 g Poly, 5.3 g Sat); 113 mg Cholesterol; 33 g Carbohydrate; 1 g Fibre; 31 g Protein; 389 mg Sodium

Beef Falafel Wraps

A meaty twist on a vegetarian favourite. Dip into Cucumber Dill Sauce, page 104, to make these even tastier.

Box of falafel mix	10 oz.	283 g
Water	1 1/4 cups	300 mL
Large egg, fork-beaten	1	1
Chopped fresh parsley (or 1 1/2 tsp., 7 mL, flakes)	2 tbsp.	30 mL
Chopped fresh mint leaves (or 3/4 tsp., 4 mL, dried)	1 tbsp.	15 mL
Lean ground beef	1 1/2 lbs.	680 g
Roasted red pepper hummus	1 cup	250 mL
Flour tortillas (9 inch, 22 cm, diameter)	8	8
Shredded lettuce, lightly packed	4 cups	1 L
Diced tomato	1 1/2 cups	375 mL

Put falafel mix into large bowl. Add water. Stir. Let stand for 15 minutes.

Add next 3 ingredients. Stir.

Add ground beef. Mix well. Divide into 24 equal portions. Shape into 3 inch (7.5 cm) diameter patties. Arrange on greased baking sheet with sides. (For other cooking methods, see page 8.) Broil on centre rack in oven for 3 to 4 minutes per side until fully cooked, and internal temperature of beef reaches 160°F (71°C).

Spread 2 tbsp. (30 mL) hummus on 1 tortilla. Layer 1/2 cup (125 mL) lettuce and 3 tbsp. (50 mL) tomato on top of hummus. Arrange 3 patties in horizontal row on top of tomato. Fold sides over filling. Roll up from bottom to enclose. Repeat to make 8 wraps.

1 wrap: 599 Calories; 26.5 g Total Fat (12.8 g Mono, 4.6 g Poly, 6.8 g Sat); 75 mg Cholesterol; 59 g Carbohydrate; 4 g Fibre; 31 g Protein; 902 mg Sodium

Pictured on page 108.

Sloppy Joe Tacos

These sloppy joes have a Mexican flair. Using tomato soup makes them quick and easy. Serve the toppings in separate bowls so guests can help themselves.

Cooking oil	2 tsp.	10 mL
Lean ground beef	1 lb.	454 g
Chopped onion	1 cup	250 mL
Can of condensed tomato soup	10 oz.	284 mL
Chili powder	1 tsp.	5 mL
Salt	3/4 tsp.	4 mL
Pepper	1/4 tsp.	1 mL
Garlic powder	1/4 tsp.	1 mL
Hard taco shells	12	12
Diced tomato	2 cups	500 mL
Shredded lettuce, lightly packed	2 cups	500 mL
Grated medium Cheddar cheese	1 cup	250 mL
Sour cream	1/2 cup	125 mL
Green onions, chopped	6	6

Heat cooking oil in large frying pan on medium. Add ground beef and onion. Scramble-fry for about 10 minutes until beef is no longer pink. Drain.

Add next 5 ingredients. Heat and stir for about 5 minutes until heated through.

Heat taco shells in oven according to package directions. Spoon beef mixture into shells. Layer remaining 5 ingredients on top of beef mixture. Makes 12 tacos.

1 taco: 211 Calories; 12.1 g Total Fat (4.5 g Mono, 1.9 g Poly, 4.8 g Sat); 34 mg Cholesterol; 15 g Carbohydrate; 2 g Fibre; 11 g Protein; 457 mg Sodium

1. Tuscan Barbecue Loaf, page 116
2. Creamy Zucchini Wedges, page 38
3. Italian Sandwich, page 102

Props courtesy of:
Cherison Enterprises Inc.
Totally Bamboo

Beef And Bean Burritos

*Simple to make, and on the table in a hurry. This is
an easy recipe to double or triple for a larger group.*

Cooking oil	2 tsp.	10 mL
Lean ground beef	1 lb.	454 g
Chopped onion	1/2 cup	125 mL
Can of refried beans	14 oz.	398 mL
Mild (or medium) salsa	1/2 cup	125 mL
Seasoned salt	1/2 tsp.	2 mL
Flour tortillas (9 inch, 22 cm, diameter)	6	6

Heat cooking oil in large frying pan on medium. Add ground beef and
onion. Scramble-fry for about 10 minutes until beef is no longer pink.
Drain.

Add next 3 ingredients. Heat and stir for about 3 minutes until
heated through.

Spoon about 1/3 cup (75 mL) beef mixture along centre of each tortilla.
Fold sides over filling. Roll up from bottom to enclose. Makes 6 burritos.

*1 burrito: 391 Calories; 16.9 g Total Fat (7.5 g Mono, 2.2 g Poly, 5.5 g Sat); 48 mg Cholesterol;
37 g Carbohydrate; 6 g Fibre; 22 g Protein; 621 mg Sodium*

1. Greek Salad Pizza, page 49
2. Cucumber Dill Sauce, page 104
3. Phyllo Lasagne, page 40
4. Beef Falafel Wraps, page 105

Props courtesy of:
Cherison Enterprises Inc.
Totally Bamboo

Thai Beef Wraps

Fragrant mint adds a fresh note to these generously filled wraps. We made four, but you can stretch the filling to make six wraps if you like.

Cooking oil	2 tsp.	10 mL
Lean ground beef	1 lb.	454 g
Garlic clove, minced (or 1/4 tsp., 1 mL, powder)	1	1
Brown sugar, packed	2 tbsp.	30 mL
Lime juice	2 tbsp.	30 mL
Finely grated, peeled gingerroot (or 3/4 tsp., 4 mL, ground ginger)	1 tbsp.	15 mL
Fish sauce (or soy sauce)	1 tbsp.	15 mL
Ground coriander	1 tsp.	5 mL
Sesame oil, for flavour	1 tsp.	5 mL
Chili paste (sambal oelek)	1 tsp.	5 mL
Fresh bean sprouts	2 cups	500 mL
Coarsely grated carrot	1 cup	250 mL
Can of sliced water chestnuts, drained and chopped	8 oz.	227 mL
Sliced green onion	1/2 cup	125 mL
Hoisin sauce	1/4 cup	60 mL
Chopped unsalted peanuts	1/4 cup	60 mL
Chopped fresh mint leaves (or cilantro), optional	2 tbsp.	30 mL
Flour tortillas (9 inch, 22 cm, diameter)	4	4

Heat cooking oil in large frying pan on medium. Add ground beef and garlic. Scramble-fry for about 10 minutes until beef is no longer pink. Drain.

Add next 7 ingredients. Heat and stir for about 2 minutes until brown sugar is dissolved.

Add next 4 ingredients. Heat and stir for about 2 minutes until vegetables are heated through. Remove from heat.

Add next 3 ingredients. Stir.

Spoon about 1 cup (250 mL) beef mixture along centre of each tortilla. Fold sides over filling. Roll up from bottom to enclose. Makes 4 wraps.

1 wrap: 534 Calories; 21.1 g Total Fat (9.7 g Mono, 4.4 g Poly, 5.2 g Sat); 59 mg Cholesterol; 58 g Carbohydrate; 5 g Fibre; 30 g Protein; 910 mg Sodium

Spiced Meatball Pitas

Appetizing and substantial, these pockets are filled with spicy meatballs that hint of Mediterranean flavours.

CUMIN LIME SAUCE

Plain yogurt	1 cup	250 mL
Grated English cucumber (with peel)	1/2 cup	125 mL
Lime juice	1 tbsp.	15 mL
Garlic clove, minced (or 1/4 tsp., 1 mL, powder)	1	1
Ground cumin	1/2 tsp.	2 mL
Salt	1/4 tsp.	1 mL
Large egg	1	1
Crushed gingersnaps	1/4 cup	60 mL
Sliced green onion	2 tbsp.	30 mL
Chopped fresh cilantro or parsley (or 1 1/2 tsp., 7 mL, dried)	2 tbsp.	30 mL
Ground cumin	1/2 tsp.	2 mL
Salt	1/2 tsp.	2 mL
Pepper	1/4 tsp.	1 mL
Ground cinnamon	1/4 tsp.	1 mL
Lean ground beef	1 lb.	454 g
Pita breads (7 inch, 18 cm, diameter)	3	3
Chopped or torn lettuce, lightly packed	1 1/2 cups	375 mL
Diced tomato	1/2 cup	125 mL
Diced green pepper	1/2 cup	125 mL

Cumin Lime Sauce: Combine first 6 ingredients in small bowl. Set aside. Makes about 1 1/2 cups (375 mL) sauce.

Combine next 8 ingredients in large bowl.

Add ground beef. Mix well. Roll into 1 inch (2.5 cm) balls. Arrange on greased baking sheet with sides. Bake in 350°F (175°C) oven for about 15 minutes until fully cooked, and internal temperature of beef reaches 160°F (71°C).

Cut pita breads in half crosswise. Fill each half with meatballs and remaining 3 ingredients. Spoon sauce over filling. Serves 6.

1 serving: 270 Calories; 8.8 g Total Fat (3.6 g Mono, 0.7 g Poly, 3.3 g Sat); 78 mg Cholesterol; 26 g Carbohydrate; 1 g Fibre; 21 g Protein; 563 mg Sodium

Teriyaki Lettuce Wraps

Tasty and fun! For a casual presentation, put topping ingredients into individual serving bowls so guests can make their own wraps. Teriyaki Sauce may be used for dipping instead of drizzling inside the wrap.

Large egg	1	1
Fine dry bread crumbs	1/3 cup	75 mL
Soy sauce	1 tbsp.	15 mL
Finely chopped green onion	1 tbsp.	15 mL
Finely grated, peeled gingerroot	1 tsp.	5 mL
(or 1/4 tsp., 1 mL, ground ginger)		
Chinese five-spice powder	1/2 tsp.	2 mL
Garlic clove, minced (or 1/4 tsp., 1 mL,	1	1
powder)		
Lean ground beef	1 lb.	454 g
TERIYAKI SAUCE		
Water	2 tsp.	10 mL
Cornstarch	2 tsp.	10 mL
Soy sauce	1/3 cup	75 mL
Brown sugar, packed	1/3 cup	75 mL
Ketchup	1/3 cup	75 mL
White vinegar	2 1/2 tbsp.	37 mL
Large green leaf lettuce leaves	12	12
Can of sliced water chestnuts, drained	8 oz.	227 mL
and finely chopped		
Grated carrot	1/2 cup	125 mL
Finely chopped green onion	1/2 cup	125 mL
Chopped fresh cilantro or parsley	1/2 cup	125 mL

Combine first 7 ingredients in large bowl.

Add ground beef. Mix well. Divide into 12 equal portions. Shape into 3 inch (7.5 cm) long logs. Place crosswise on greased wire rack set on baking sheet with sides. (For other cooking methods, see page 8.) Broil on centre rack in oven for about 20 minutes, turning once at halftime, until fully cooked, and internal temperature of beef reaches 160°F (71°C). Cool.

(continued on next page)

Teriyaki Sauce: Stir water and cornstarch in small cup until smooth.

Combine next 4 ingredients in small saucepan. Bring to a boil on medium. Slowly add cornstarch mixture, stirring constantly. Heat and stir for about 3 minutes until boiling and thickened. Cool. Makes about 1 cup (250 mL) sauce.

Place 1 beef log crosswise in centre of 1 lettuce leaf. Drizzle with about 1 tbsp. (15 mL) Teriyaki Sauce.

Sprinkle about 2 tsp. (10 mL) of each remaining ingredient over log. Fold sides of leaf over filling. Roll up from bottom to enclose. Repeat to make 12 wraps.

1 wrap: 157 Calories; 6.4 g Total Fat (2.7 g Mono, 0.4 g Poly, 2.5 g Sat); 39 mg Cholesterol; 15 g Carbohydrate; 1 g Fibre; 10 g Protein; 718 mg Sodium

Paré Pointer

Then there are the bankers: they chain up their pens and leave the doors open.

Curried Yam Empanadas

Pop the frozen dinner roll dough in your refrigerator in the morning, and you'll have these meal-sized turnovers done for dinner in no time.

Cooking oil	2 tsp.	10 mL
Extra-lean ground beef	1 lb.	454 g
Finely diced peeled yam	1 cup	250 mL
Finely chopped onion	1/2 cup	125 mL
Curry powder	1/2 tsp.	2 mL
Ground cumin	1/2 tsp.	2 mL
Salt	1/2 tsp.	2 mL
Pepper	1/2 tsp.	2 mL
Ground cinnamon	1/4 tsp.	1 mL
Ground cloves	1/8 tsp.	0.5 mL
Dried cranberries	1/4 cup	60 mL
Chopped slivered almonds, toasted (see Tip, page 129)	1/4 cup	60 mL
Ketchup	3 tbsp.	50 mL
Lime juice	2 tbsp.	30 mL
Chili paste (sambal oelek)	1 tsp.	5 mL
Frozen unbaked dinner rolls, covered, thawed in refrigerator	8	8
Large egg, fork-beaten	1	1

Heat cooking oil in large frying pan on medium. Add next 9 ingredients. Scramble-fry for about 10 minutes until ground beef is no longer pink and yam is tender. Drain. Transfer to medium bowl.

Add next 5 ingredients. Stir. Cool.

Roll out 1 dough portion on lightly floured surface to 6 inch (15 cm) diameter disc. Spoon about 1/3 cup (75 mL) beef mixture onto disc, leaving 1/2 inch (12 mm) edge. Fold dough over beef mixture. Crimp edges with fork to seal. Place on greased baking sheet. Repeat with remaining dough and beef mixture.

Brush tops and sides of empanadas with egg. Bake in 375°F (190°C) oven for about 20 minutes until golden. Let stand on baking sheet for 5 minutes before serving. Makes 8 empanadas.

1 empanada: 295 Calories; 14.8 g Total Fat (7.2 g Mono, 1.6 g Poly, 4.4 g Sat); 59 mg Cholesterol; 26 g Carbohydrate; 3 g Fibre; 15 g Protein; 412 mg Sodium

Chutney Beef Scones

A tender, golden scone infused with great curry flavour.
Serve this with tomato or mushroom soup for lunch!

Cooking oil	1 tsp.	5 mL
Lean ground beef	1/2 lb.	225 g
Chopped onion	1/4 cup	60 mL
Curry powder	1 tsp.	5 mL
All-purpose flour	2 cups	500 mL
Baking powder	1 tbsp.	15 mL
Baking soda	1/2 tsp.	2 mL
Salt	1/2 tsp.	2 mL
Cold hard margarine (or butter), cut up	1/4 cup	60 mL
Large eggs	2	2
Milk	3/4 cup	175 mL
Grated Swiss cheese	1/2 cup	125 mL
Mango chutney, larger pieces finely chopped	1/4 cup	60 mL

Heat cooking oil in medium frying pan on medium. Add ground beef, onion and curry powder. Scramble-fry for about 10 minutes until beef is no longer pink. Drain. Cool.

Stir next 4 ingredients in large bowl. Cut in margarine until mixture resembles coarse crumbs. Add beef mixture. Stir. Make a well in centre.

Combine remaining 4 ingredients in small bowl. Add to well. Stir until just moistened. Spread evenly in greased 9 inch (22 cm) round pan. Bake in 350°F (175°C) oven for about 30 minutes until golden and wooden pick inserted in centre comes out clean. Let stand in pan for 10 minutes before removing to wire rack to cool. Cuts into 12 wedges. Serves 6.

1 serving: 386 Calories; 17.1 g Total Fat (8.6 g Mono, 1.7 g Poly, 5.4 g Sat); 101 mg Cholesterol; 40 g Carbohydrate; 2 g Fibre; 17 g Protein; 663 mg Sodium

Tuscan Barbecue Loaf

Serve this grilled loaf with salad for a simple summertime supper. Perfect patio fare.

Large egg	1	1
Chopped fresh white mushrooms	1 cup	250 mL
Chopped onion	1/2 cup	125 mL
Grated zucchini (with peel)	1/2 cup	125 mL
Fine dry bread crumbs	1/2 cup	125 mL
Tomato sauce	1/2 cup	125 mL
Roasted red peppers, drained, blotted dry, finely chopped	1/4 cup	60 mL
Basil pesto	2 tbsp.	30 mL
Garlic clove, minced (or 1/4 tsp., 1 mL, powder)	1	1
Extra-lean ground beef	1 1/2 lbs.	680 g
French bread loaf	1	1
Grated Asiago cheese	1 cup	250 mL
Chopped pine nuts, toasted (see Tip, page 129)	1/2 cup	125 mL
Chopped fresh parsley (or 3/4 tsp., 4 mL, flakes)	1 tbsp.	15 mL

Combine first 9 ingredients in large bowl.

Add ground beef. Mix well.

Cut bread loaf in half horizontally. Spread beef mixture evenly on both halves. Place each half on separate sheet of heavy-duty foil. Bring foil up over sides of bread, leaving tops uncovered. Place on baking sheet. Preheat gas barbecue to medium. Place baking sheet on grill. Close lid. Cook for about 40 minutes until fully cooked.

Sprinkle with remaining 3 ingredients. Cook for another 3 to 5 minutes until cheese is melted. Cut each half into 3 pieces, for a total of 6 pieces.

1 piece: 600 Calories; 27.1 g Total Fat (10.7 g Mono, 4.8 g Poly, 9 g Sat); 110 mg Cholesterol; 53 g Carbohydrate; 6 g Fibre; 38 g Protein; 826 mg Sodium

Pictured on page 107.

Creamy Pepper Quesadillas

Extra-crispy tortilla wedges are stuffed with a creamy Tex-Mex filling.
The chipotle chili pepper gives them a delightfully spicy flavour.

Cooking oil	2 tsp.	10 mL
Lean ground beef	1 lb.	454 g
Finely chopped green pepper	1/4 cup	60 mL
Roasted red peppers, drained, blotted dry, finely chopped	1/4 cup	60 mL
Chipotle chili pepper in adobo sauce, finely chopped (see Tip, page 74)	1	1
Chili powder	1 tsp.	5 mL
Ground cumin	1/2 tsp.	2 mL
Pepper	1/2 tsp.	2 mL
Block of cream cheese, softened	8 oz.	250 g
Flour tortillas (9 inch, 22 cm, diameter)	8	8
Grated Monterey Jack cheese	2 cups	500 mL
Cooking oil	1 tbsp.	15 mL

Heat first amount of cooking oil in large frying pan on medium. Add ground beef. Scramble-fry for about 10 minutes until no longer pink. Drain.

Add next 6 ingredients. Heat and stir for about 2 minutes until fragrant and green pepper is tender-crisp. Remove from heat.

Spread about 2 tbsp. (30 mL) cream cheese on each tortilla. Sprinkle Monterey Jack cheese over 1/2 of cream cheese. Scatter beef mixture over Monterey Jack cheese. Fold tortillas over filling. Press down lightly.

Brush both sides of folded tortillas with second amount of cooking oil. Arrange on 2 greased baking sheets. Bake on separate racks in 400°F (205°C) oven for about 15 minutes, switching position of baking sheets at halftime, until crisp and cheese is melted. Cut each quesadilla into 3 wedges, for a total of 24 wedges. Serves 8.

1 serving: 473 Calories; 30.6 g Total Fat (10.7 g Mono, 2.9 g Poly, 15.1 g Sat); 90 mg Cholesterol; 25 g Carbohydrate; 2 g Fibre; 24 g Protein; 479 mg Sodium

Layered Taco Salad

This salad can be made ahead and refrigerated overnight. Use a glass bowl for best visual impact. Serve with your favourite tortilla chips.

Cooking oil	2 tsp.	10 mL
Lean ground beef	1 lb.	454 g
Finely chopped onion	1/2 cup	125 mL
Taco seasoning mix, stir before measuring	2 tbsp.	30 mL
Mayonnaise	3/4 cup	175 mL
Sour cream	1/2 cup	125 mL
Chopped fresh cilantro or parsley	2 tbsp.	30 mL
Lime juice	2 tbsp.	30 mL
Taco seasoning mix, stir before measuring	1 tbsp.	15 mL
Shredded romaine lettuce, lightly packed	3 1/2 cups	875 mL
Shredded iceberg lettuce, lightly packed	2 1/2 cups	625 mL
Mild salsa	1 cup	250 mL
Chopped yellow or green pepper	1 cup	250 mL
Chopped tomato	1 1/2 cups	375 mL
Grated medium Cheddar cheese	1/2 cup	125 mL
Can of sliced ripe olives, drained	4 1/2 oz.	125 mL
Chopped green onion	1/4 cup	60 mL

Heat cooking oil in large frying pan on medium. Add ground beef and onion. Scramble-fry for about 10 minutes until beef is no longer pink. Drain.

Add first amount of taco seasoning. Heat and stir for 1 minute. Transfer to medium bowl. Cover. Chill until cold.

Combine next 5 ingredients in separate medium bowl. Set aside.

Combine romaine and iceberg lettuce in large serving bowl. Scatter beef mixture over lettuce.

Layer next 3 ingredients, in order given, on top of beef mixture. Spread mayonnaise mixture on top of tomato to side of bowl to seal.

Sprinkle remaining 3 ingredients over top. Serves 8.

1 serving: 357 Calories; 29 g Total Fat (14.3 g Mono, 6.7 g Poly, 6.6 g Sat); 56 mg Cholesterol; 11 g Carbohydrate; 2 g Fibre; 14 g Protein; 931 mg Sodium

Pictured on page 126.

Norway Spinach Salad

Norwegian Gjetost (pronounced YEHT-ohst) cheese has a smooth,
fudge-like texture and a slightly sweet taste that is unequalled.
This salad is sure to impress your guests!

CREAMY CHÈVRE DRESSING

Mayonnaise	1/4 cup	60 mL
Apple juice	3 tbsp.	50 mL
Goat (chèvre) cheese	1 1/2 oz.	43 g
Apple cider vinegar	1 tbsp.	15 mL
Dry mustard	1/4 tsp.	1 mL
Pepper	1/4 tsp.	1 mL
Cooking oil	2 tsp.	10 mL
Lean ground beef	1 lb.	454 g
Ground allspice	3/4 tsp.	4 mL
Salt	1/2 tsp.	2 mL
Pepper	1/4 tsp.	1 mL
Bag of fresh spinach, stems removed	10 oz.	284 g
Shaved Gjetost (or smoked Gouda) cheese	4 1/2 oz.	125 g
Medium cooking apples (such as McIntosh), with peel and sliced	2	2

Creamy Chèvre Dressing: Process first 6 ingredients in blender or food processor until smooth. Makes about 2/3 cup (150 mL) dressing.

Heat cooking oil in large frying pan on medium. Add next 4 ingredients. Scramble-fry for about 10 minutes until ground beef is no longer pink. Drain. Cool.

Arrange spinach on 4 dinner plates. Top with beef, Gjetost cheese and apple slices. Drizzle with dressing. Serves 4.

1 serving: 513 Calories; 35.8 g Total Fat (15.2 g Mono, 5.4 g Poly, 12.7 g Sat); 111 mg Cholesterol; 16 g Carbohydrate; 3 g Fibre; 33 g Protein; 779 mg Sodium

Caribbean Beef Salad

*Doesn't this take you to the tropics? The lime, coconut dressing
and mild jerk spices bring this salad to life.*

Brown sugar, packed	1/3 cup	75 mL
Dried thyme	1 tsp.	5 mL
Ground ginger	3/4 tsp.	4 mL
Ground cinnamon	1/2 tsp.	2 mL
Ground allspice	1/2 tsp.	2 mL
Ground nutmeg	1/4 tsp.	1 mL
Ground coriander	1/4 tsp.	1 mL
Salt	1/4 tsp.	1 mL
Cayenne pepper	1/4 tsp.	1 mL
Coconut milk (or reconstituted from powder)	1/4 cup	60 mL
Corn syrup (or liquid honey)	2 tbsp.	30 mL
Mayonnaise	2 tbsp.	30 mL
Lime juice	1 tbsp.	15 mL
Large egg	1	1
Medium unsweetened coconut, toasted (see Tip, page 129)	1/2 cup	125 mL
Coconut milk (or reconstituted from powder)	1/3 cup	75 mL
Garlic clove, minced (or 1/4 tsp., 1 mL, powder)	1	1
Pepper	1/4 tsp.	1 mL
Lean ground beef	1 lb.	454 g
Chopped or torn romaine lettuce, lightly packed	4 cups	1 L
Small red onion, halved lengthwise and thinly sliced	1	1
Cubed mango	2 cups	500 mL
Small red pepper, cut into 1 inch (2.5 cm) pieces	1	1
Sultana raisins	1/4 cup	60 mL

(continued on next page)

Plain cashews	1/4 cup	60 mL
Medium unsweetened coconut, toasted (see Tip, page 129)	2 tbsp.	30 mL
Lime wedges, for garnish		

Combine first 9 ingredients in shallow dish. Transfer 1 tsp. (5 mL) to small bowl.

Add next 4 ingredients to spice mixture in small bowl. Stir. Set aside.

Combine next 5 ingredients in medium bowl.

Add ground beef. Mix well. Divide into 16 equal portions. Shape into 1/2 inch (12 mm) thick patties. Press both sides of each patty into spice mixture in shallow dish. Arrange on greased baking sheet with sides. Broil on top rack in oven for 5 to 7 minutes per side until fully cooked, and internal temperature of beef reaches 160°F (71°C).

Arrange lettuce on 4 dinner plates. Scatter next 4 ingredients over top. Place 4 patties on each salad. Drizzle with coconut milk mixture.

Sprinkle with cashews and second amount of coconut.

Garnish with lime wedges. Serves 4.

1 serving: 687 Calories; 38.5 g Total Fat (11.2 g Mono, 3.5 g Poly, 20.8 g Sat); 115 mg Cholesterol; 65 g Carbohydrate; 5 g Fibre; 27 g Protein; 300 mg Sodium

Pictured on front cover.

Paré Pointer

It's put on the table and someone cuts it, but never eats it.
What is it? A deck of cards!

Continental Rice Salad

*Cooking the ground beef with dill weed gives this salad
its deliciously unique flavour. Definitely one to try!*

Cooking oil	2 tsp.	10 mL
Lean ground beef	1 lb.	454 g
Chopped onion	1/2 cup	125 mL
Dill weed	1/2 tsp.	2 mL
Cooked converted white rice (about 1 cup, 250 mL, uncooked)	3 cups	750 mL
PARSLEY PEPPERCORN DRESSING		
Olive (or cooking) oil	3 tbsp.	50 mL
Chopped fresh parsley	3 tbsp.	50 mL
White wine vinegar	1 tbsp.	15 mL
Whole green peppercorns, drained and crushed	1 tbsp.	15 mL
Paprika	1/2 tsp.	2 mL
Salt	1/4 tsp.	1 mL
Medium tomatoes, each cut into 8 wedges	3	3
English cucumber (with peel), halved lengthwise and cut into 1/4 inch (6 mm) slices	2 cups	500 mL
Diced green pepper	1 cup	250 mL
Can of artichoke hearts, drained and quartered (optional)	14 oz.	398 mL

Heat cooking oil in large frying pan on medium. Add ground beef, onion
and dill weed. Scramble-fry for about 10 minutes until beef is no longer
pink. Drain. Remove from heat.

Add rice. Stir. Transfer to extra-large bowl. Cover. Chill for about 2 hours
until cold.

Parsley Peppercorn Dressing: Combine first 6 ingredients in jar with
tight-fitting lid. Shake well. Makes about 1/3 cup (75 mL) dressing.

Add remaining 4 ingredients to beef mixture. Stir. Drizzle with dressing.
Stir. Serves 6.

1 serving: 390 Calories; 20.3 g Total Fat (11 g Mono, 1.7 g Poly, 5.7 g Sat); 42 mg Cholesterol;
34 g Carbohydrate; 2 g Fibre; 18 g Protein; 357 mg Sodium

Pictured on page 126.

Cheesy Meatball Salad

Crunchy meatballs add interesting texture to this salad made for cheese lovers. The tangy dressing goes great with pasta, too.

PARSLEY PESTO DRESSING

Coarsely chopped fresh parsley	1/2 cup	125 mL
Grated Parmesan cheese	1/3 cup	75 mL
Olive (or cooking) oil	1/3 cup	75 mL
Pine nuts, toasted (see Tip, page 129)	1/4 cup	60 mL
Red wine vinegar	1/4 cup	60 mL
Garlic clove, minced (or 1/4 tsp., 1 mL, powder)	1	1
Salt	1/4 tsp.	1 mL
Pepper	1/8 tsp.	0.5 mL
Grated medium Cheddar cheese	1 1/2 cups	375 mL
Biscuit mix	1/2 cup	125 mL
Seasoned salt	1/2 tsp.	2 mL
Pepper, just a pinch		
Lean ground beef	1/2 lb.	225 g
Bag of mixed salad greens	4 1/2 oz.	128 g
Fresh spinach, stems removed, lightly packed	1 cup	250 mL
Thinly sliced red onion	1/2 cup	125 mL

Parsley Pesto Dressing: Process first 8 ingredients in blender or food processor until smooth. Makes about 2/3 cup (150 mL) dressing.

Combine next 4 ingredients in medium bowl.

Add ground beef. Mix well. Roll into 1 inch (2.5 cm) balls. Arrange on greased baking sheet with sides. Bake in 400°F (205°C) oven for 10 to 15 minutes until fully cooked, and internal temperature of beef reaches 160°F (71°C). Transfer to paper towels to drain. Cover to keep warm.

Arrange salad greens on 6 salad plates. Top with meatballs, spinach and onion. Drizzle with dressing. Serves 6.

1 serving: 413 Calories; 32.8 g Total Fat (15.9 g Mono, 3.7 g Poly, 11.2 g Sat); 55 mg Cholesterol; 12 g Carbohydrate; 2 g Fibre; 20 g Protein; 658 mg Sodium

Hearty Wild Rice Soup

Earthy mushrooms and a pleasant hint of tarragon complement the nutty flavour of wild rice. Delicious.

Cooking oil	2 tsp.	10 mL
Chopped fresh white mushrooms	2 cups	500 mL
Lean ground beef	1 lb.	454 g
Chopped onion	1 cup	250 mL
Dried tarragon leaves	1 tsp.	5 mL
All-purpose flour	3 tbsp.	50 mL
Prepared beef broth	6 cups	1.5 L
Wild rice	2/3 cup	150 mL
Grated carrot	1/2 cup	125 mL

Heat cooking oil in large pot or Dutch oven on medium. Add next 4 ingredients. Scramble-fry for about 10 minutes until ground beef is no longer pink. Drain.

Add flour. Stir well. Add broth and rice. Stir until boiling. Reduce heat to medium-low. Simmer, covered, for about 50 minutes, stirring occasionally, until rice is tender.

Add carrot. Heat and stir for about 2 minutes until carrot is tender-crisp. Skim any fat from surface of soup. Makes about 8 cups (2 L).

1 cup (250 mL): 187 Calories; 6.6 g Total Fat (2.9 g Mono, 0.7 g Poly, 2.2 g Sat); 29 mg Cholesterol; 16 g Carbohydrate; 2 g Fibre; 15 g Protein; 646 mg Sodium

1. Portuguese Soup, page 132
2. Mexican Beef Soup, page 133
3. Hearty Mushroom Soup, page 130

Props courtesy of: Casa Bugatti
Pier 1 Imports
Stokes
The Bay
Totally Bamboo

Potato Fennel Soup

This rich, hearty soup is loaded with vegetables.
Fennel and dill add a refreshing, light flavour.

Cooking oil	2 tsp.	10 mL
Sliced fennel bulb (white part only)	2 cups	500 mL
Lean ground beef	1 lb.	454 g
Diced carrot	1 cup	250 mL
Chopped onion	1/2 cup	125 mL
Prepared beef broth	6 cups	1.5 L
Diced peeled potato	2 cups	500 mL
Chopped fresh dill (or 1/2 tsp., 2 mL, dill weed)	2 tsp.	10 mL
Pepper	1/4 tsp.	1 mL

Heat cooking oil in large pot or Dutch oven on medium. Add next
4 ingredients. Scramble-fry for about 10 minutes until ground beef is
no longer pink. Drain.

Add remaining 4 ingredients. Stir. Bring to a boil. Boil gently, covered, for
about 15 minutes, stirring occasionally, until potato is tender. Skim any fat
from surface of soup. Makes about 9 cups (2.25 L).

1 cup (250 mL): 143 Calories; 5.7 g Total Fat (2.6 g Mono, 0.5 g Poly, 1.9 g Sat);
26 mg Cholesterol; 11 g Carbohydrate; 1 g Fibre; 12 g Protein; 595 mg Sodium

1. Layered Taco Salad, page 118
2. Continental Rice Salad, page 122
3. Chèvre Beef Salad, page 128

Props courtesy of: Cherison Enterprises Inc.
Strahl
The Dazzling Gourmet
Totally Bamboo

Chèvre Beef Salad

*Creamy goat cheese accents savoury beef patties in
a colourful full-meal salad your guests will love.*

BASIL VINAIGRETTE

Chopped fresh basil	1/2 cup	125 mL
Olive (or cooking) oil	1/3 cup	75 mL
White wine vinegar	1/4 cup	60 mL
Dried oregano	1/2 tsp.	2 mL
Salt, sprinkle		
Pepper, sprinkle		
Large egg	1	1
White bread slice, processed into crumbs	1	1
Balsamic vinegar	2 tbsp.	30 mL
Dried oregano	1 tsp.	5 mL
Garlic clove, minced (or 1/4 tsp., 1 mL, powder)	1	1
Salt	1/8 tsp.	0.5 mL
Pepper, sprinkle		
Lean ground beef	1 lb.	454 g
Cooking oil	2 tsp.	10 mL
Mixed salad greens, lightly packed	8 cups	2 L
Thinly sliced English cucumber (with peel)	3/4 cup	175 mL
Cherry tomatoes, halved	16	16
Thinly sliced yellow pepper	1/2 cup	125 mL
Goat (chèvre) cheese, cut up	4 oz.	113 g

Basil Vinaigrette: Process first 6 ingredients in blender or food processor until smooth. Makes about 3/4 cup (175 mL) vinaigrette.

Combine next 7 ingredients in large bowl.

Add ground beef. Mix well. Divide into 8 equal portions. Shape into 1/2 inch (12 mm) thick oval patties.

Heat cooking oil in large frying pan on medium. (For other cooking methods, see page 8.) Add patties. Cook for about 5 minutes per side until fully cooked, and internal temperature of beef reaches 160°F (71°C). Transfer to paper towels to drain. Let stand for 5 minutes. Cut each patty into 4 pieces.

(continued on next page)

Soups & Salads

Arrange salad greens on 4 dinner plates. Scatter cucumber, tomato and yellow pepper over greens.

Top each salad with 8 patty pieces. Scatter goat cheese over top. Drizzle with vinaigrette. Serves 4.

1 serving: 545 Calories; 41.2 g Total Fat (22 g Mono, 3.7 g Poly, 12.8 g Sat); 135 mg Cholesterol; 14 g Carbohydrate; 3 g Fibre; 32 g Protein; 348 mg Sodium

Pictured on page 126.

 To toast nuts, seeds or coconut, place them in an ungreased shallow frying pan. Heat on medium for 3 to 5 minutes, stirring often, until golden. To bake, spread them evenly in an ungreased shallow pan. Bake in a 350°F (175°C) oven for 5 to 10 minutes, stirring or shaking often, until golden.

Paré Pointer

If you want to light up your yard, plant bulbs.

Hearty Mushroom Soup

Ground beef and pretty pastry "croutons" make this velvety mushroom soup substantial enough to be a meal in itself.

PUFFED TRIANGLES

Package of frozen puff pastry (14 oz., 397 g), thawed according to package directions	1/2	1/2
Large egg, fork-beaten	1	1
Cooking oil	1 tsp.	5 mL
Lean ground beef	1 lb.	454 g
Chopped fresh white mushrooms	5 1/2 cups	1.4 L
Finely chopped onion	2 cups	500 mL
Garlic clove, minced (or 1/4 tsp., 1 mL, powder)	1	1
Prepared beef broth	3 2/3 cups	900 mL
Can of condensed cream of mushroom soup	10 oz.	284 mL
Dry sherry	1/2 cup	125 mL
Chopped fresh tarragon leaves (or 3/4 tsp., 4 mL, dried)	1 tbsp.	15 mL
Salt	1/4 tsp.	1 mL
Pepper	1/8 tsp.	0.5 mL
Sour cream	1 cup	250 mL
Chopped fresh tarragon leaves	2 tbsp.	30 mL

Puffed Triangles: Roll out puff pastry on lightly floured surface to 8 inch (20 cm) square. Brush with egg. Cut pastry lengthwise into thirds, then crosswise into quarters, for a total of 12 rectangles. Cut each rectangle in half diagonally, for a total of 24 triangles. Arrange in single layer on parchment paper-lined baking sheet. Bake in 400°F (205°C) oven for about 15 minutes until puffed and golden. Cool. Makes 24 triangles.

Heat cooking oil in large pot or Dutch oven on medium. Add ground beef. Scramble-fry for about 10 minutes until no longer pink. Drain.

Add next 3 ingredients. Cook for 5 to 10 minutes, stirring often, until onion is softened.

(continued on next page)

Soups & Salads

Add next 6 ingredients. Stir. Bring to a boil. Boil gently, uncovered, for 20 minutes, stirring occasionally.

Add sour cream. Heat and stir until hot but not boiling. Ladle into 8 soup bowls. Top each with 3 Puffed Triangles. Sprinkle with second amount of tarragon. Serves 8.

1 serving: 372 Calories; 23 g Total Fat (6.7 g Mono, 7.5 g Poly, 7 g Sat); 69 mg Cholesterol; 22 g Carbohydrate; 2 g Fibre; 17 g Protein; 867 mg Sodium

Pictured on page 125.

Italian Meatball Soup

This tasty soup is a creative way to serve pasta with meatballs.

Large egg	1	1
Crushed seasoned croutons	1/4 cup	60 mL
Chopped fresh parsley (or 1 1/2 tsp., 7 mL, flakes)	2 tbsp.	30 mL
Grated Parmesan cheese	2 tbsp.	30 mL
Garlic clove, minced (or 1/4 tsp., 1 mL, powder)	1	1
Lean ground beef	1 lb.	454 g
Prepared beef broth	7 cups	1.75 L
Very small pasta (such as orzo or alpha)	2/3 cup	150 mL
Finely shredded basil	2 tbsp.	30 mL

Combine first 5 ingredients in medium bowl.

Add ground beef. Mix well. Roll into 3/4 inch (2 cm) balls. Arrange on greased baking sheet with sides. Bake in 350°F (175°C) oven for about 15 minutes until fully cooked, and internal temperature of beef reaches 160°F (71°C). Transfer to paper towels to drain. Set aside.

Measure broth into large pot or Dutch oven. Bring to a boil on high. Add pasta. Stir. Reduce heat to medium. Boil gently, uncovered, for 5 to 6 minutes until pasta is tender but firm.

Add meatballs and basil. Heat and stir for about 1 minute until meatballs are heated through. Makes about 8 cups (2 L).

1 cup (250 mL): 209 Calories; 7.1 g Total Fat (2.9 g Mono, 0.5 g Poly, 2.8 g Sat); 58 mg Cholesterol; 18 g Carbohydrate; 1 g Fibre; 17 g Protein; 817 mg Sodium

Portuguese Soup

Adjust this soup to suit your taste. Sprinkle individual servings
with grated Parmesan cheese for added flavour.

Lean ground beef	1/2 lb.	225 g
Chorizo (or hot Italian) sausages, casings removed, chopped	1/2 lb.	225 g
Cooking oil	2 tsp.	10 mL
Chopped onion	3 cups	750 mL
Garlic clove, minced (or 1/4 tsp., 1 mL, powder)	1	1
Low-sodium prepared chicken broth	6 cups	1.5 L
Diced potato (with peel)	3 cups	750 mL
Can of white kidney beans, rinsed and drained	19 oz.	540 mL
Pepper	1/4 tsp.	1 mL
Green kale (see Note), stems removed, chopped, lightly packed	4 cups	1 L

Put ground beef and sausage into medium bowl. Mix well.

Heat cooking oil in large pot or Dutch oven on medium. Add beef mixture, onion and garlic. Scramble-fry for about 10 minutes until meat is no longer pink. Drain.

Add next 4 ingredients. Stir. Bring to a boil on medium-high. Reduce heat to medium-low. Simmer, covered, for about 10 minutes, stirring occasionally, until potato is tender.

Add kale. Cook for about 10 minutes, stirring occasionally, until tender. Makes about 11 1/2 cups (2.9 L).

1 cup (250 mL): 162 Calories; 5.1 g Total Fat (2.3 g Mono, 0.7 g Poly, 1.6 g Sat); 17 mg Cholesterol; 19 g Carbohydrate; 4 g Fibre; 11 g Protein; 493 mg Sodium

Pictured on page 125.

Note: Instead of kale, the same amount of spinach may be used. Spinach cooks much faster than kale. After adding spinach to the soup, cook only for 1 to 2 minutes until spinach is just wilted.

Mexican Beef Soup

Pair this mildly seasoned soup with cornbread muffins or tossed salad.

Cooking oil	2 tsp.	10 mL
Lean ground beef	1 lb.	454 g
Chopped onion	1 cup	250 mL
Chopped green pepper	1 cup	250 mL
Garlic clove, minced (or 1/4 tsp., 1 mL, powder)	1	1
Water	4 cups	1 L
Can of mixed beans, rinsed and drained	19 oz.	540 mL
Can of condensed tomato soup	10 oz.	284 mL
Can of condensed Cheddar cheese soup	10 oz.	284 mL
Taco seasoning mix, stir before measuring	2 tbsp.	30 mL
Can of diced green chilies (optional)	4 oz.	113 g
Sour cream	1 cup	250 mL
Sour cream, for garnish		
Chopped fresh cilantro or parsley, for garnish		

Heat cooking oil in large pot or Dutch oven on medium. Add next 4 ingredients. Scramble-fry for about 10 minutes until ground beef is no longer pink. Drain.

Add next 6 ingredients. Stir. Bring to a boil. Reduce heat to medium-low. Simmer, uncovered, for 15 minutes, stirring occasionally, to blend flavours.

Add first amount of sour cream. Heat and stir until hot but not boiling.

Garnish individual servings with a dollop of sour cream and a sprinkle of cilantro. Makes about 10 cups (2.5 L).

1 cup (250 mL): 221 Calories; 11.4 g Total Fat (4 g Mono, 1 g Poly, 5.4 g Sat); 40 mg Cholesterol; 17 g Carbohydrate; 2 g Fibre; 13 g Protein; 945 mg Sodium

Pictured on page 125.

Sweet Lentil Curry

*Accompany this gently sweet curry with a refreshing
cucumber salad to complement its mild spiciness.*

Cooking oil	2 tsp.	10 mL
Lean ground beef	1 lb.	454 g
Chopped onion	1/2 cup	125 mL
Diced celery	1/2 cup	125 mL
Curry powder	1 tsp.	5 mL
Dried thyme	1/2 tsp.	2 mL
Ground cumin	1/2 tsp.	2 mL
Pepper	1/2 tsp.	2 mL
Ground cinnamon	1/4 tsp.	1 mL
Can of diced tomatoes (with juice)	14 oz.	398 mL
Cubed peeled sweet potato (or yam)	1 1/2 cups	375 mL
Dried red lentils	1 cup	250 mL
Water	1 cup	250 mL
Frozen concentrated apple juice	1/4 cup	60 mL
Diced peeled apple	1 cup	250 mL
Lemon juice	1 tbsp.	15 mL
Liquid honey	2 tsp.	10 mL

Heat cooking oil in large saucepan or Dutch oven on medium. Add next
8 ingredients. Scramble-fry for about 10 minutes until ground beef is no
longer pink. Drain.

Add next 5 ingredients. Stir. Bring to a boil. Reduce heat to medium-low.
Simmer, covered, for about 25 minutes, stirring occasionally, until lentils
are tender.

Combine apple, lemon juice and honey. in small bowl. Add to beef
mixture. Stir. Simmer, covered, for another 5 minutes until apple is
softened. Serves 4.

*1 serving: 515 Calories; 13 g Total Fat (5.6 g Mono, 1.5 g Poly, 4 g Sat); 59 mg Cholesterol;
65 g Carbohydrate; 9 g Fibre; 37 g Protein; 240 mg Sodium*

Stovetop Dishes

Macaroni Jumble

Kids will love this! Easy to make for supper when there's not a lot of time.

Elbow macaroni	2 cups	500 mL
Cooking oil	2 tsp.	10 mL
Lean ground beef	1 lb.	454 g
Chopped onion	1/3 cup	75 mL
Frozen kernel corn (or 12 oz., 341 mL, can of kernel corn, drained)	1 1/2 cups	375 mL
Can of tomato sauce	7 1/2 oz.	213 mL
Ketchup	1/2 cup	125 mL
Water	1/2 cup	125 mL
Chili powder	2 tsp.	10 mL
Granulated sugar	1/2 tsp.	2 mL
Seasoned salt	1/2 tsp.	2 mL
Grated medium Cheddar cheese	1/2 cup	125 mL

Cook macaroni in boiling salted water in large uncovered saucepan for 8 to 10 minutes, stirring occasionally, until tender but firm. Drain. Set aside.

Heat cooking oil in large frying pan on medium. Add ground beef and onion. Scramble-fry for about 10 minutes until beef is no longer pink. Drain.

Add next 7 ingredients. Heat and stir for about 1 minute until boiling. Reduce heat to medium-low. Simmer, uncovered, for 8 to 10 minutes, stirring occasionally, until slightly thickened. Add macaroni. Heat and stir for about 5 minutes until heated through.

Sprinkle with cheese. Remove from heat. Let stand for about 1 minute until cheese is melted. Serves 4.

1 serving: 576 Calories; 18.5 g Total Fat (7.2 g Mono, 1.9 g Poly, 7.2 g Sat); 74 mg Cholesterol; 70 g Carbohydrate; 5 g Fibre; 35 g Protein; 1013 mg Sodium

Pictured on page 144.

Salisbury Steak

Tender, well-seasoned meat patties are smothered in mushroom sauce.

Fine dry bread crumbs	1/4 cup	60 mL
Finely chopped onion	1/4 cup	60 mL
Water	1/4 cup	60 mL
Celery salt	1/2 tsp.	2 mL
Pepper	1/4 tsp.	1 mL
Garlic powder	1/4 tsp.	1 mL
Dry mustard	1/4 tsp.	1 mL
Lean ground beef	1 lb.	454 g
Cooking oil	2 tsp.	10 mL
MUSHROOM SAUCE		
Prepared beef broth	1/4 cup	60 mL
All-purpose flour	2 tbsp.	30 mL
Prepared beef broth	1 cup	250 mL
Can of sliced mushrooms, drained	10 oz.	284 mL
Worcestershire sauce	1/2 tsp.	2 mL
Dried thyme	1/4 tsp.	1 mL

Combine first 7 ingredients in medium bowl.

Add ground beef. Mix well. Divide into 4 equal portions. Shape into 3/4 inch (2 cm) thick oval patties.

Heat cooking oil in large frying pan on medium. Add patties. Cook for about 5 minutes per side until fully cooked, and internal temperature of beef reaches 160°F (71°C). Remove to large serving platter. Cover to keep warm. Discard drippings, reserving any brown bits in pan.

Mushroom Sauce: Blend first amount of broth with flour in small cup. Set aside.

Slowly pour second amount of broth into same pan on medium, stirring constantly and scraping any brown bits from bottom of pan.

Add remaining 3 ingredients. Stir. Stir flour mixture. Slowly add to mushroom mixture, stirring constantly. Heat and stir for about 5 minutes until boiling and thickened. Makes about 1 1/2 cups (375 mL) sauce. Spoon over patties. Serves 4.

1 serving: 256 Calories; 12.5 g Total Fat (5.8 g Mono, 1.2 g Poly, 4.1 g Sat); 59 mg Cholesterol; 11 g Carbohydrate; 2 g Fibre; 24 g Protein; 670 mg Sodium

Pictured on page 144.

Ginger Beef

Ground beef as ginger beef? You bet! Delicious over chow mein noodles.

Water	2/3 cup	150 mL
Oyster sauce	1/4 cup	60 mL
Granulated sugar	1 tbsp.	15 mL
Cornstarch	2 tsp.	10 mL
Beef bouillon powder	1 tsp.	5 mL
Sesame oil, for flavour	1 tsp.	5 mL
Dried crushed chilies	1/2 tsp.	2 mL
Cornstarch	2 tbsp.	30 mL
Soy sauce	1 tbsp.	15 mL
Finely grated, peeled gingerroot	2 tsp.	10 mL
Garlic clove, minced (or 1/4 tsp., 1 mL, powder)	1	1
Onion powder	1/4 tsp.	1 mL
Extra-lean ground beef	1 lb.	454 g
Cooking oil	1 tbsp.	15 mL
Thinly sliced green pepper	1 cup	250 mL
Green onions, cut into 1/2 inch (12 mm) pieces	6	6

Combine first 7 ingredients in small bowl. Set aside.

Combine next 5 ingredients in medium bowl.

Add ground beef. Mix well.

Heat cooking oil in large frying pan on medium. Add beef mixture. Stir. Cook for about 10 minutes, coarsely breaking up beef, until no longer pink. Drain.

Add green pepper and onion. Heat and stir for 2 minutes. Stir oyster sauce mixture. Add to beef mixture. Heat and stir for about 1 minute until boiling and thickened. Serves 4.

1 serving: 396 Calories; 20.7 g Total Fat (9.5 g Mono, 2.2 g Poly, 6.7 g Sat); 92 mg Cholesterol; 17 g Carbohydrate; 1 g Fibre; 34 g Protein; 1485 mg Sodium

Pictured on page 143.

Sukiyaki Rice Bowl

No need to order in when Asian flavour is what
you're craving. This dish will satisfy!

Water	3 tbsp.	50 mL
Cornstarch	2 tbsp.	30 mL
Cooking oil	2 tsp.	10 mL
Extra-lean ground beef	1 lb.	454 g
Cooking oil	2 tsp.	10 mL
Large onion, halved lengthwise and sliced	1	1
Sliced fresh white mushrooms	1 1/2 cups	375 mL
Shredded suey choy (Chinese cabbage), lightly packed	2 cups	500 mL
Thinly sliced carrot	1 cup	250 mL
Can of bamboo shoots, drained	8 oz.	227 mL
Low-sodium soy sauce	1/2 cup	125 mL
Apple juice	1/2 cup	125 mL
Water	1/2 cup	125 mL
Granulated sugar	2 tbsp.	30 mL
Beef bouillon powder	1 tsp.	5 mL
Green onions, cut into 1 inch (2.5 cm) pieces	4	4
Hot cooked long grain white rice (about 1 1/3 cups, 325 mL, uncooked)	4 cups	1 L

Sliced green onion, for garnish

Stir first amount of water, and cornstarch in small cup until smooth. Set aside.

Heat first amount of cooking oil in large frying pan on medium. Add ground beef. Scramble-fry for about 10 minutes until no longer pink. Drain. Transfer to medium bowl. Cover to keep warm.

Heat second amount of cooking oil in same pan. Add onion and mushrooms. Cook for 5 to 10 minutes, stirring often, until onion is softened.

Add next 9 ingredients. Stir. Cook, covered, for 2 to 3 minutes until boiling. Add beef. Stir. Stir cornstarch mixture. Add to beef mixture. Heat and stir for 1 to 2 minutes until boiling and thickened.

(continued on next page)

Spoon rice into individual bowls. Spoon beef mixture over rice.

Garnish with second amount of green onion. Serves 6.

1 serving: 486 Calories; 14.3 g Total Fat (6.6 g Mono, 1.6 g Poly, 4.6 g Sat); 61 mg Cholesterol; 59 g Carbohydrate; 3 g Fibre; 28 g Protein; 868 mg Sodium

Pictured on page 143.

Moroccan-Style Beef

A tasty blend of honey and spices complements the slightly sweet fruit flavours in this dish. Serve with couscous for a traditional North African meal.

Cooking oil	1 tsp.	5 mL
Lean ground beef	1 lb.	454 g
Chopped onion	1 1/2 cups	375 mL
Chopped dried apricot	1 cup	250 mL
Chopped dried pitted prunes (or raisins)	1/2 cup	125 mL
All-purpose flour	2 tbsp.	30 mL
Ground cumin	2 tsp.	10 mL
Ground cinnamon	1/2 tsp.	2 mL
Prepared beef broth	4 cups	1 L
Lemon juice	2 tbsp.	30 mL
Liquid honey	1 tbsp.	15 mL
Grated lemon zest	1 tsp.	5 mL
Chopped fresh parsley (or 3/4 tsp., 4 mL, flakes)	1 tbsp.	15 mL

Heat cooking oil in large frying pan on medium. Add ground beef and onion. Scramble-fry for about 10 minutes until beef is no longer pink. Drain.

Add next 5 ingredients. Stir well. Slowly add broth, stirring constantly. Bring to a boil. Reduce heat to medium-low. Simmer, uncovered, for about 20 minutes, stirring occasionally, until sauce is thickened and fruit is softened.

Add next 3 ingredients. Stir. Remove to large serving bowl.

Sprinkle with parsley. Serves 4.

1 serving: 401 Calories; 12.4 g Total Fat (5.3 g Mono, 0.8 g Poly, 4.2 g Sat); 57 mg Cholesterol; 50 g Carbohydrate; 6 g Fibre; 26 g Protein; 894 mg Sodium

Ground Beef Curry

Lots of colour in this flavourful, mild curry. If you've never used sambal oelek before, here's a good place to start. If you're already a fan, add as much as you like.

Cooking oil	1 tsp.	5 mL
Lean ground beef	1 lb.	454 g
Chopped onion	1 cup	250 mL
Garlic clove, minced (or 1/4 tsp., 1 mL, powder)	1	1
All-purpose flour	2 tbsp.	30 mL
Curry powder	2 tbsp.	30 mL
Prepared beef broth	1 1/2 cups	375 mL
Tomato juice	1 1/4 cups	300 mL
Can of chickpeas (garbanzo beans), rinsed and drained	14 oz.	398 mL
Diced tomato	1 1/2 cups	375 mL
Frozen peas, thawed	1 cup	250 mL
Salt	1/4 tsp.	1 mL
Chili paste (sambal oelek), optional	1/2 – 1 tsp.	2 – 5 mL
Plain yogurt	1/2 cup	125 mL
Chopped fresh cilantro or parsley, for garnish		

Heat cooking oil in large frying pan on medium. Add ground beef and onion. Scramble-fry for about 10 minutes until beef is no longer pink. Drain.

Add garlic. Heat and stir for 1 to 2 minutes until fragrant.

Add flour and curry powder. Heat and stir for 1 minute.

Slowly add broth, stirring constantly. Add tomato juice and chickpeas. Stir until boiling. Boil gently, uncovered, for about 15 minutes, stirring occasionally, until thickened.

Add next 4 ingredients. Stir. Cook for about 5 minutes, stirring occasionally, until peas are heated through. Remove from heat.

(continued on next page)

Add yogurt. Stir well. Remove to large serving bowl.

Garnish with cilantro. Serves 6.

1 serving: 262 Calories; 9.2 g Total Fat (3.7 g Mono, 1 g Poly, 3 g Sat); 39 mg Cholesterol; 24 g Carbohydrate; 4 g Fibre; 21 g Protein; 671 mg Sodium

Pictured on page 72.

Five-Spice Hot Pot

Chinese five-spice powder gives this Asian-style dish its distinct flavour. Pair with rice or spring rolls.

Cooking oil	2 tsp.	10 mL
Lean ground beef	1 lb.	454 g
Chopped onion	1/2 cup	125 mL
Garlic clove, minced (or 1/4 tsp., 1 mL, powder)	1	1
Fresh stir-fry vegetable mix	4 cups	1 L
Cans of tomato sauce (14 oz., 398 mL, each)	2	2
Shredded suey choy (Chinese cabbage), lightly packed	2 cups	500 mL
Can of sliced water chestnuts, drained	8 oz.	227 mL
Soy sauce	3 tbsp.	50 mL
Chili powder	1 tsp.	5 mL
Chinese five-spice powder	1/2 tsp.	2 mL
Fresh bean sprouts	1/2 cup	125 mL
Thinly sliced green onion	2 tbsp.	30 mL

Heat cooking oil in large frying pan or wok on medium. Add ground beef, onion and garlic. Scramble-fry for about 10 minutes until beef is no longer pink. Drain.

Add next 7 ingredients. Stir. Bring to a boil. Reduce heat to medium-low. Simmer, uncovered, for about 15 minutes, stirring occasionally, until vegetables are tender-crisp. Remove to large serving bowl.

Sprinkle with bean sprouts and green onion. Serves 6.

1 serving: 230 Calories; 8.6 g Total Fat (3.8 g Mono, 0.9 g Poly, 2.7 g Sat); 38 mg Cholesterol; 22 g Carbohydrate; 4 g Fibre; 19 g Protein; 1434 mg Sodium

Pictured on page 71.

Country Hash Skillet

Thick gravy coats this mildly seasoned beef hash.
A one-dish meal that's on the table in no time.

Cooking oil	2 tsp.	10 mL
Lean ground beef	1 lb.	454 g
Chopped onion	1 cup	250 mL
Chopped celery	1/4 cup	60 mL
All-purpose flour	2 tbsp.	30 mL
Beef bouillon powder	1 tbsp.	15 mL
Celery salt	1/2 tsp.	2 mL
Onion powder	1/2 tsp.	2 mL
Water	1 1/4 cups	300 mL
Frozen hash brown potatoes	2 cups	500 mL
Frozen mixed vegetables	1 1/2 cups	375 mL

Heat cooking oil in large frying pan on medium. Add ground beef, onion and celery. Scramble-fry for about 10 minutes until beef is no longer pink. Drain.

Add next 4 ingredients. Stir. Add water. Heat and stir for about 1 minute until boiling and thickened.

Add potatoes and vegetables. Cook for about 10 minutes, stirring occasionally, until heated through. Serves 4.

1 serving: 365 Calories; 12.9 g Total Fat (5.6 g Mono, 1.5 g Poly, 4.2 g Sat); 59 mg Cholesterol; 37 g Carbohydrate; 5 g Fibre; 26 g Protein; 695 mg Sodium

1. Ginger Beef, page 137
2. Sukiyaki Rice Bowl, page 138
3. Beef With Basil, page 149

Props courtesy of: Casa Bugatti
Cherison Enterprises Inc.
Island Pottery
Out of the Fire Studio

No-Fuss Stroganoff

*A delicious stovetop classic that made its debut
in Casseroles. Spoon over egg noodles or
mashed potatoes for a hearty meal.*

Hard margarine (or butter)	2 tbsp.	30 mL
Lean ground beef	1 lb.	454 g
Finely chopped onion	1 cup	250 mL
All-purpose flour	2 tbsp.	30 mL
Pepper	1/4 tsp.	1 mL
Can of sliced mushrooms, drained	10 oz.	284 mL
Can of condensed cream of chicken soup	10 oz.	284 mL
Sour cream	1/2 cup	125 mL
Grated medium Cheddar cheese	1/4 cup	60 mL

Melt margarine in large frying pan on medium. Add ground beef and onion.
Scramble-fry for about 10 minutes until beef is no longer pink. Drain.

Add flour and pepper. Stir well. Add mushrooms. Heat and stir for 2 minutes.

Add soup. Stir. Cook, uncovered, for 10 minutes, stirring occasionally.

Add sour cream and cheese. Heat and stir for 2 to 3 minutes until heated
through and cheese is melted. Serves 4.

*1 serving: 491 Calories; 35.6 g Total Fat (14.2 g Mono, 4.3 g Poly, 13.8 g Sat); 84 mg Cholesterol;
16 g Carbohydrate; 2 g Fibre; 27 g Protein; 989 mg Sodium*

1. Macaroni Jumble, page 135
2. Porcupine Stew, page 64
3. Salisbury Steak, page 136

Props courtesy of: Canhome Global
Casa Bugatti
Emile Henry

Fruity Beef Curry

An attractive, fragrant curry with fantastic flavour! Serve over rice or couscous.

Ingredient	Imperial	Metric
Cooking oil	2 tsp.	10 mL
Lean ground beef	1 lb.	454 g
Salt	1 tsp.	5 mL
Chopped onion	1 1/2 cups	375 mL
Cumin seed	1 tbsp.	15 mL
Coarsely grated, peeled gingerroot	2 tsp.	10 mL
(or 1/2 tsp., 2 mL, ground ginger)		
Turmeric	1 tsp.	5 mL
Ground cardamom	1/2 tsp.	2 mL
Bay leaf	1	1
Ground cloves	1/8 tsp.	0.5 mL
Dried crushed chilies (optional)	1/2 tsp.	2 mL
Medium tomatoes, seeds removed, chopped	3	3
Medium cooking apples (such as McIntosh), peeled and each cut into 6 wedges	2	2
Juice and grated peel of 1 medium lemon, 1/2 of grated peel reserved		
Sultana raisins	1/2 cup	125 mL
Medium bananas, cut into 1 inch (2.5 cm) pieces	2	2
Chopped ripe mango	1 cup	250 mL
Liquid honey	2 tbsp.	30 mL
Raw cashews, toasted (see Tip, page 129)	1/3 cup	75 mL
Reserved grated lemon peel		

Heat cooking oil in large frying pan on medium. Add ground beef and salt. Scramble-fry for about 10 minutes until beef is no longer pink. Drain.

Add next 8 ingredients. Stir. Cook for about 5 minutes, stirring often, until onion is softened.

Add next 4 ingredients. Stir. Cook, covered, for about 5 minutes, stirring twice, until apple just starts to soften.

(continued on next page)

Add banana, mango and honey. Stir. Cook, covered, for 1 to 2 minutes until heated through and fruit is slightly softened. Discard bay leaf.

Sprinkle individual servings with cashews and reserved lemon peel. Serves 4.

1 serving: 534 Calories; 18.8 g Total Fat (8.9 g Mono, 2.3 g Poly, 5.2 g Sat); 59 mg Cholesterol; 73 g Carbohydrate; 7 g Fibre; 26 g Protein; 656 mg Sodium

Paré Pointer

He jumped off the roof into a pool of cola but wasn't hurt because it was a soft drink.

Saucy Skillet Dinner

Family-friendly, and one of our favourites from One-Dish Meals. A thick, rich sauce coats spaghetti in this delicious dinner.

Cooking oil	2 tsp.	10 mL
Lean ground beef	1 lb.	454 g
Chopped onion	1 cup	250 mL
Garlic clove, minced (or 1/4 tsp., 1 mL, powder)	1	1
Medium zucchini (with peel), halved lengthwise and sliced	1	1
Chopped fresh white mushrooms	1 cup	250 mL
Tomato pasta sauce	2 cups	500 mL
Water	1 cup	250 mL
Dried basil	1/2 tsp.	2 mL
Granulated sugar	1/2 tsp.	2 mL
Dried whole oregano, just a pinch		
Spaghetti, broken into 1 – 2 inch (2.5 – 5 cm) pieces	6 oz.	170 g
Grated part-skim mozzarella cheese	1/2 cup	125 mL

Heat cooking oil in large frying pan on medium. Add ground beef, onion and garlic. Scramble-fry for about 10 minutes until beef is no longer pink. Drain.

Add zucchini and mushrooms. Cook for 6 to 7 minutes, stirring occasionally, until vegetables are softened.

Add next 5 ingredients. Stir. Bring to a boil.

Add spaghetti. Stir. Reduce heat to medium-low. Simmer, covered, for about 20 minutes until spaghetti is tender but firm and liquid is almost absorbed.

Add cheese. Stir until melted. Serves 4.

1 serving: 537 Calories; 16.6 g Total Fat (6.6 g Mono, 2 g Poly, 5.9 g Sat); 66 mg Cholesterol; 65 g Carbohydrate; 9 g Fibre; 36 g Protein; 226 mg Sodium

Beef With Basil

A wonderful mingling of aromatic sauces and spices gives
ground beef an exotic flavour. Best served with rice.

Cooking oil	2 tsp.	10 mL
Lean ground beef	1 lb.	454 g
Cooking oil	1 tbsp.	15 mL
Medium carrots, thinly sliced diagonally	2	2
Cubed green pepper	1 cup	250 mL
Chopped onion	1/2 cup	125 mL
Fresh chili pepper (see Tip, page 47), minced (or 1/2 tsp., 2 mL, dried crushed chilies)	1	1
Garlic clove, minced (or 1/4 tsp., 1 mL, powder)	1	1
Water	1/2 cup	125 mL
Chili sauce	1/3 cup	75 mL
Soy sauce	1 tbsp.	15 mL
Fish sauce (or soy sauce)	1 tbsp.	15 mL
Ground cinnamon	1/2 tsp.	2 mL
Granulated sugar	1/2 tsp.	2 mL
Chopped fresh basil	1/2 cup	125 mL

Heat first amount of cooking oil in large frying pan on medium. Add ground beef. Scramble-fry for about 10 minutes until no longer pink. Drain. Transfer to medium bowl. Set aside.

Heat second amount of cooking oil in same pan. Add next 5 ingredients. Cook for 3 to 4 minutes, stirring often, until vegetables are tender-crisp.

Add beef and next 6 ingredients. Stir. Reduce heat to low. Cook, uncovered, for 20 to 30 minutes, stirring occasionally, until thickened.

Add basil. Stir. Serves 4.

1 serving: 299 Calories; 15.5 g Total Fat (7.6 g Mono, 2.2 g Poly, 4.2 g Sat); 59 mg Cholesterol; 17 g Carbohydrate; 4 g Fibre; 23 g Protein; 902 mg Sodium

Pictured on page 143.

Measurement Tables

Throughout this book measurements are given in Conventional and Metric measure. To compensate for differences between the two measurements due to rounding, a full metric measure is not always used. The cup used is the standard 8 fluid ounce. Temperature is given in degrees Fahrenheit and Celsius. Baking pan measurements are in inches and centimetres as well as quarts and litres. An exact metric conversion is given below as well as the working equivalent (Metric Standard Measure).

Spoons

Conventional Measure	Metric Exact Conversion Millilitre (mL)	Metric Standard Measure Millilitre (mL)
1/8 teaspoon (tsp.)	0.6 mL	0.5 mL
1/4 teaspoon (tsp.)	1.2 mL	1 mL
1/2 teaspoon (tsp.)	2.4 mL	2 mL
1 teaspoon (tsp.)	4.7 mL	5 mL
2 teaspoons (tsp.)	9.4 mL	10 mL
1 tablespoon (tbsp.)	14.2 mL	15 mL

Cups

Conventional Measure	Metric Exact Conversion Millilitre (mL)	Metric Standard Measure Millilitre (mL)
1/4 cup (4 tbsp.)	56.8 mL	60 mL
1/3 cup (5 1/3 tbsp.)	75.6 mL	75 mL
1/2 cup (8 tbsp.)	113.7 mL	125 mL
2/3 cup (10 2/3 tbsp.)	151.2 mL	150 mL
3/4 cup (12 tbsp.)	170.5 mL	175 mL
1 cup (16 tbsp.)	227.3 mL	250 mL
4 1/2 cups	1022.9 mL	1000 mL (1 L)

Oven Temperatures

Fahrenheit (°F)	Celsius (°C)
175°	80°
200°	95°
225°	110°
250°	120°
275°	140°
300°	150°
325°	160°
350°	175°
375°	190°
400°	205°
425°	220°
450°	230°
475°	240°
500°	260°

Dry Measurements

Conventional Measure Ounces (oz.)	Metric Exact Conversion Grams (g)	Metric Standard Measure Grams (g)
1 oz.	28.3 g	28 g
2 oz.	56.7 g	57 g
3 oz.	85.0 g	85 g
4 oz.	113.4 g	125 g
5 oz.	141.7 g	140 g
6 oz.	170.1 g	170 g
7 oz.	198.4 g	200 g
8 oz.	226.8 g	250 g
16 oz.	453.6 g	500 g
32 oz.	907.2 g	1000 g (1 kg)

Pans

Conventional Inches	Metric Centimetres
8x8 inch	20x20 cm
9x9 inch	22x22 cm
9x13 inch	22x33 cm
10x15 inch	25x38 cm
11x17 inch	28x43 cm
8x2 inch round	20x5 cm
9x2 inch round	22x5 cm
10x4 1/2 inch tube	25x11 cm
8x4x3 inch loaf	20x10x7.5 cm
9x5x3 inch loaf	22x12.5x7.5 cm

Casseroles

CANADA & BRITAIN		UNITED STATES	
Standard Size Casserole	Exact Metric Measure	Standard Size Casserole	Exact Metric Measure
1 qt. (5 cups)	1.13 L	1 qt. (4 cups)	900 mL
1 1/2 qts. (7 1/2 cups)	1.69 L	1 1/2 qts. (6 cups)	1.35 L
2 qts. (10 cups)	2.25 L	2 qts. (8 cups)	1.8 L
2 1/2 qts. (12 1/2 cups)	2.81 L	2 1/2 qts. (10 cups)	2.25 L
3 qts. (15 cups)	3.38 L	3 qts. (12 cups)	2.7 L
4 qts. (20 cups)	4.5 L	4 qts. (16 cups)	3.6 L
5 qts. (25 cups)	5.63 L	5 qts. (20 cups)	4.5 L

Recipe Index

155

Company's Coming cookbooks are available at retail locations throughout Canada!

EXCLUSIVE mail order offer on next page

Buy any 2 cookbooks—choose a 3rd FREE of equal or lesser value than the lowest price paid.

Original Series $15.99

CODE		CODE		CODE	
SQ	150 Delicious Squares	CCLFC	Low-Fat Cooking	PD	Potluck Dishes
CA	Casseroles	SCH	Stews, Chilies & Chowders	GBR	Ground Beef Recipes
MU	Muffins & More	FD	Fondues	FRIR	4-Ingredient Recipes
SA	Salads	CCBE	The Beef Book	KHC	Kids' Healthy Cooking
AP	Appetizers	RC	The Rookie Cook	MM	Mostly Muffins
CO	Cookies	RHR	Rush-Hour Recipes	SP	Soups
PA	Pasta	SW	Sweet Cravings	SU	Simple Suppers
BA	Barbecues	YRG	Year-Round Grilling	CCDC	Diabetic Cooking
PR	Preserves	GG	Garden Greens	CHN	Chicken Now
CH	Chicken, Etc.	CHC	Chinese Cooking	KDS	Kids Do Snacks
CT	Cooking For Two	RL	Recipes For Leftovers	TMRC	30-Minute Rookie Cook
SC	Slow Cooker Recipes	BEV	The Beverage Book	LFE	Low-Fat Express
SF	Stir-Fry	SCD	Slow Cooker Dinners	SI	Choosing Sides
MAM	Make-Ahead Meals	WM	30-Minute Weekday Meals	PAS	Perfect Pasta And Sauces
PB	The Potato Book	SDL	School Days Lunches	TMDC	30-Minute Diabetic Cooking NEW *October 15/08*

Cookbook Author Biography

CODE	$15.99
JP	Jean Paré: An Appetite for Life

Most Loved Recipe Collection

CODE	$23.99
MLBQ	Most Loved Barbecuing
MLCO	Most Loved Cookies

CODE	$24.99
MLSD	Most Loved Salads & Dressings
MLCA	Most Loved Casseroles
MLSF	Most Loved Stir-Fries
MLHF	Most Loved Holiday Favourites
MLSC	Most Loved Slow Cooker Creations
MLDE	Most Loved Summertime Desserts NEW *April 1/08*

3-in-1 Cookbook Collection

CODE	$29.99
MNT	Meals in No Time
MME	Meals Made Easy NEW *July 1/08*

Practical Gourmet – NEW!

CODE	$29.99
SPFS	Small Plates for Sharing NEW *Sept. 1/08*

Lifestyle Series

CODE	$17.99
DC	Diabetic Cooking

CODE	$19.99
DDI	Diabetic Dinners
HR	Easy Healthy Recipes
HH	Healthy in a Hurry
WGR	Whole Grain Recipes

Special Occasion Series

CODE	$20.99
GFK	Gifts from the Kitchen

CODE	$24.99
MLBQ	Christmas Gifts from the Kitchen
TR	Timeless Recipes for All Occasions
CCT	Company's Coming–Tonight! NEW *Oct. 1/08*

CODE	$27.99
CCEL	Christmas Celebrations

CODE	$29.99
CATH	Cooking At Home

Order ONLINE for fast delivery!

Log onto **www.companyscoming.com**, browse through our library of cookbooks, gift sets and newest releases and place your order using our fast and secure online order form.

Buy 2, Get 1 FREE!

Buy any 2 cookbooks—choose a **3rd FREE** of equal or lesser value than the lowest price paid.

Title	Code	Quantity	Price	Total
			$	$

DON'T FORGET to indicate your FREE BOOK(S). (see exclusive mail order offer above) PLEASE PRINT

TOTAL BOOKS (including FREE)

TOTAL BOOKS PURCHASED:

	INTERNATIONAL via Air Mail	USA	Canada
Shipping & Handling First Book (per destination)	$ 32.98 (one book)	$ 9.98 (one book)	$ 5.98 (one book)
Additional Books (include FREE books)	$ ($7.99 each)	$ ($1.99 each)	$ ($1.99 each)
Sub-Total	$	$	$
Canadian residents add GST/HST			$
TOTAL AMOUNT ENCLOSED	$	$	$

Terms

- All orders must be prepaid. Sorry, no CODs.
- Canadian orders are processed in Canadian funds, US International orders. are processed in US Funds.
- Prices are subject to change without prior notice.
- Canadian residents must pay GST/HST (no provincial tax required).
- No tax is required for orders outside Canada.
- Satisfaction is guaranteed or return within 30 days for a full refund.
- Make cheque or money order payable to: **Company's Coming Publishing Limited** 2311-96 Street, Edmonton, Alberta Canada T6N 1G3.
- Orders are shipped surface mail. For courier rates, visit our website: **www.companyscoming.com** or contact us: **Tel: 780-450-6223 Fax: 780-450-1857.**

Gift Giving

- Let us help you with your gift giving!
- We will send cookbooks directly to the recipients of your choice if you give us their names and addresses.
- Please specify the titles you wish to send to each person.
- If you would like to include a personal note or card, we will be pleased to enclose it with your gift order.
- Company's Coming Cookbooks make excellent gifts: birthdays, bridal showers, Mother's Day, Father's Day, graduation or any occasion …collect them all!

☐ MasterCard ☐ VISA Expiry ____ / ____ MO/YR

Credit Card # _____

Name of cardholder _____

Cardholder signature _____

Shipping Address Send the cookbooks listed above to:

☐ **Please check if this is a Gift Order**

Name: _____

Street: _____

City: _____ Prov./State: _____

Postal Code/Zip: _____ Country: _____

Tel: (____) _____

E-mail address: _____

Your privacy is important to us. We will not share your e-mail address or personal information with any outside party.

☐ **YES! Please add me to your News Bite e-mail newsletter.**

Cookmark

We focused on creating recipes for a diabetic lifestyle, but we also focused on designing delicious dishes the whole family would love—all on the table in 30 minutes or less. Eating well has never been simpler!

COOKBOOKS

Quick
&
Easy
Recipes

Everyday
Ingredients

Canada's
**most popular
cookbooks!**

Complete your Original Series Collection!

- ❏ 150 Delicious Squares
- ❏ Casseroles
- ❏ Muffins & More
- ❏ Salads
- ❏ Appetizers
- ❏ Cookies
- ❏ Pasta
- ❏ Barbecues
- ❏ Preserves
- ❏ Chicken, Etc.
- ❏ Cooking For Two
- ❏ Slow Cooker Recipes
- ❏ Stir-Fry
- ❏ Make-Ahead Meals
- ❏ The Potato Book
- ❏ Low-Fat Cooking
- ❏ Stews, Chilies & Chowders
- ❏ Fondues
- ❏ The Beef Book
- ❏ The Rookie Cook
- ❏ Rush-Hour Recipes
- ❏ Sweet Cravings
- ❏ Year-Round Grilling
- ❏ Garden Greens
- ❏ Chinese Cooking
- ❏ Recipes For Leftovers
- ❏ The Beverage Book
- ❏ Slow Cooker Dinners
- ❏ 30-Minute Weekday Meals
- ❏ School Days Lunches
- ❏ Potluck Dishes
- ❏ Ground Beef Recipes
- ❏ 4-Ingredient Recipes
- ❏ Kids' Healthy Cooking
- ❏ Mostly Muffins
- ❏ Soups
- ❏ Simple Suppers
- ❏ Diabetic Cooking
- ❏ Chicken Now
- ❏ Kids Do Snacks
- ❏ 30-Minute Rookie Cook
- ❏ Low-Fat Express
- ❏ Choosing Sides
- ❏ Perfect Pasta And Sauces
- ❏ 30-Minute Diabetic Cooking **NEW** *October 15/08*

FREE Online NEWSLETTER

- **FREE** recipes & cooking tips
- **Exclusive** cookbook offers
- **Preview** new titles

Subscribe today!

www.companyscoming.com

COLLECT ALL Company's Coming Series Cookbooks!

Most Loved Recipe Collection

- ❏ Most Loved Barbecuing
- ❏ Most Loved Cookies
- ❏ Most Loved Salads & Dressings
- ❏ Most Loved Casseroles
- ❏ Most Loved Stir-Fries
- ❏ Most Loved Holiday Favourites
- ❏ Most Loved Slow Cooker Creations
- ❏ Most Loved Summertime Desserts **NEW** *April 1/08*

Lifestyle Series

- ❏ Diabetic Cooking
- ❏ Diabetic Dinners
- ❏ Easy Healthy Recipes
- ❏ Whole Grain Recipes

Canada's most popular cookbooks!

Practical Gourmet

- ❏ Small Plates for Sharing **NEW** *Sept. 1/08*

Special Occasion Series

- ❏ Gifts from the Kitchen
- ❏ Christmas Gifts from the Kitchen
- ❏ Timeless Recipes for All Occasions
- ❏ Christmas Celebrations
- ❏ Cooking at Home
- ❏ Company's Coming—Tonight! **NEW** *October 1/08*

Cookbook Author Biography

- ❏ Jean Paré: An Appetite for Life

3-in-1 Cookbook Collection

- ❏ Meals in No Time
- ❏ Meals Made Easy **NEW** *July 1/08*